Clem Sunter

What it *really* takes to be World Class

HUMAN & ROUSSEAU
TAFELBERG

First published in 1997 jointly by
Human & Rousseau (Pty) Ltd, State House,
3-9 Rose Street, Cape Town
and Tafelberg Publishers Ltd, 28 Wale Street, Cape Town

First edition, first impression 1997
Second impression 1997
ISBN 0 7981 3758 4

TO ALLAN NEWEY
AND THE ANGLO SCENARIO TEAM
IN LONDON
They blazed the trail in identifying
that the global economy is now in a "long boom",
as the hottest magazine in the US – *Wired* –
calls it in its July 1997 edition. Anyone betting
on Chart 20 in my book *The New Century* (1992)
and on Charts 38 and 39 in
The High Road: Where are we now? (1996)
would have made a fortune on the
stock exchange. All these charts point out
that we're in the upswing cycle of
the 5th Kondratieff wave which is due to
last until 2020. Allan and his team
are definitely world class.

ACKNOWLEDGEMENTS

This book owes a great deal to David Wightman. As editor of the *Sunday Tribune,* he invited me some three years ago to write a weekly column. I felt honoured to accept this task because I have always had a high regard for "The Trib". More than that, David was my mentor who gave me clear and sensible advice when I needed it most. Jonathan Hobday, formerly editor of the *Sunday Argus,* subsequently decided to feature my weekly column in his newspaper too. I was just as proud of that.

I have consistently followed one principle as a columnist: try to write on something different every week so that the readers are kept guessing as to what "Sunter on Sunday" is going to contain until they open the centre page. Nevertheless, I love writing about excellence whenever I come across it. So it was relatively easy to put together a collection of my articles under the umbrella *What It Really Takes To Be World Class*. The date of publication is given at the beginning of each article.

I have identified seven attributes which are keys to being world class: uniqueness; focus; global orientation; innovation; a sensitive radar system; the ability to attract talented young people; and social and environmental responsibility.

The book demonstrates that some combination of these attributes applies across a broad range of fields. I have covered business, government, the economy, cities, sport and individuals. In particular, I believe that South Africa has every chance of developing into a world-class economy since it has already shown the talent and commitment to join the ranks of world-class sporting nations.

I must thank my secretary, Pat Meneghini, for typing and collating my articles so efficiently. I'm also truly grateful to my customary publishing team of Linette Viljoen, Jill Martin and Jürgen Fomm. Jürgen has as usual come up with a spectacular cover design to attract the attention of browsers in bookshops. I hope they find the content pleasing as well.

CONTENTS

The 5 x 10 x 10 rule

To be a world-class company, you need to pass a written as well as an oral examination. The written one concerns financial statistics. The first written test is to grow your real earnings per share at a minimum of 5 per cent per annum over ten years and offer shareholders a total real return of at least 10 per cent per annum over the same period. Notice the word "real". One must strip inflation out of the financial figures because the high inflation rate in South Africa has tended to make corporate results look more satisfactory than they really are. Shareholders are only interested in what they can buy with the "real" money they make. Increasingly they are voicing this concern at the annual general meetings of the companies in which they have invested. Shareholder democracy is gaining ground everywhere. One proviso is that the behaviour of any share is to a certain extent subject to the general fluctuations of the market. For sure, though, world-class companies beat the index over the long haul.

6.4.1997 An interim report of the reputable *World Competitiveness Yearbook* shows South Africa has slid to second last among the 46 industrialised countries listed. Only Russia was behind South Africa. The US, Singapore, Hong Kong and Finland occupied the top four places.

This is probably as good a time as any to review what a world-class company really means. Because one rule of the game has changed forever for South Africa. We are now an open economy with all the opportunities and threats that go with such status. If we don't nurture world-class companies, we will remain at the bottom of the class.

Equally, with the relaxing of exchange controls and concurrent widening of investment opportunities, a South African pension fund or unit trust is increasingly going to compare South African companies with the likes of General Electric in the US and British Airways in the UK, i.e. world-class companies overseas. The locals will therefore have to perform according to world-class norms of performance to attract or retain their local as well as their overseas shareholders.

The bottom-line norm by which we will be judged I call the 5x10x10 rule. A world-class company should grow its earnings per share at an average of at least 5 per cent per annum in real terms over ten years ("real" means taking the inflationary element out of the earnings). Over the same period, it should offer its shareholders at least a 10 per cent total annual return – again in real terms. The return is calculated by purchasing the company's shares ten years ago, re-investing all the intervening dividends in the share as they are paid out and selling the enlarged shareholding today.

Now I say "at least" because the really good American companies have exceeded these targets and I'm merely using the median figures quoted for the *Fortune 500* companies. For example, looking at earnings per share growth in real terms over ten years, Caterpillar and Gillette achieved 15 per cent, Merck and Quaker Oats 17 per cent, Walt Disney 20 per cent, Motorola 30 per cent, Dow Chemical and Nike 40 per cent and Intel a whopping 114 per cent. Turning to total annual returns to investors in real terms over ten years, Kimberley-Clark and Reebok yielded 18 per cent, Pepsico as well as Johnson & Johnson 20 per cent, Philip Morris 24 per cent, Coca-Cola 25 per cent, Compaq Computer 32 per cent and Home Depot 40 per cent.

To put these figures in the context of South Africa, our inflation rate is currently around 9 per cent per annum. Thus to hit the basic target of 5 per cent growth in real terms in earnings per share and 10 per cent for total annual return, South African companies will have to achieve 14 per cent and 19 per cent respectively in nominal terms. That is pretty breathtaking stuff. Retrospectively, only a handful of companies here can boast that kind of track record.

To get anywhere in life, you have to set yourself a measurable target and regularly monitor progress. I believe the first thing we should do in an attempt to become a world-class economy is make the 5x10x10 rule a baseline for South African industry. Lists of companies should be regularly compiled in order to see who is above and below this dividing line. However, there's more to being world class than just being a success to your shareholders. It actually requires you to be regarded as a success by all your stakeholders, which extends the constituency to both employees and the public in addition to the investment community.

MVA/EVA

The second written test to qualify as a world-class company is to achieve market value-added and economic value-added ratios which are consistently positive. The economic value-added ratio can also be used with great effect to ascertain whether one part of your business is cross-subsidising another. In the right hands, EVA can be as potent as Peron!

4.5.1997   Apart from value as a long-term investment and financial soundness, another yardstick is used nowadays to judge whether a company can be considered financially world class. It's the use of corporate assets. There are two ratios employed to measure this: market value-added (MVA) and economic value-added (EVA).

MVA looks at how much shareholder wealth has been enlarged or obliterated over the life of a company. One adds up all the money investors have put in, including equity and debt offerings, loans from the bank, retained earnings and research and development spending, and compares the total with the company's current market capitalisation, i.e. what the shareholders can in aggregate take out today. A positive figure means long-term wealth creation and a negative figure long-term wealth destruction. According to the December 9 edition of *Fortune*, top of the 1996 list in America is unsurprisingly Coca-Cola with an MVA of $87,8 billion. General Electric follows at $80,8 billion. Merck ($63,4 billion), Philip Morris ($51,6 billion) and Microsoft ($44,9 billion) occupy the next three places.

At the bottom end of the chart lie IBM with a negative figure of minus $5,9 billion, General Motors (minus $8,2 billion), RJR Nabisco (minus $11,9 billion) and Ford Motor (minus $12,9 billion). One of the reasons the automotive companies fare so badly on this list is that they are sitting on huge cash balances. General Motors has nearly $12 billion and Ford $9 billion. Whilst there is every good reason to have substantial reserves for product development and capital spending, the problem is that the interest on cash balances offers a relatively low return. This has an adverse impact on MVAs.

The second statistic, EVA, is a shorter-term measure. It simply compares the company's after-tax profit with an imputed cost of capital (both borrowed and equity) on an annual basis. Studies have shown that a company that racks up a positive EVA year after year will see its MVA soar, while negative EVA will drag down MVA as the market loses faith that the company will ever provide a decent return on invested capital. The top five companies on the MVA rating all have highly positive EVAs: Coke at $2,1 billion, GE at $1,9 billion, Merck at $1,1 billion, Philip Morris at $1,2 billion and Microsoft at $1,3 billion. Intel which is No. 12 on the MVA list has the strongest EVA at $2,4 billion.

Interestingly, the *Fortune* article which lists all the MVAs and EVAs also provides the return on capital that these world-class companies are obtaining together with their cost of capital. Coke's return compared to its cost is 37,2 per cent versus 12 per cent; GE's is 17,5 per cent versus 13,5 per cent; and Microsoft's 50 per cent versus 13,1 per cent.

To put these figures in a South African context, take GE's cost of capital of 13,5 per cent. The gilt-edged bond rate in the US last year was 6,5 per cent so the risk premium for GE is 7 per cent. In South Africa our bond rates are 15 per cent, so by adding GE's premium we get to a minimum target of 22 per cent. That is a fairly awesome figure for a return on capital here and demonstrates that we can learn a trick or two from the Americans on how to deploy capital effectively. A recent survey in fact indicated that the US has an unchallenged lead in the world in capital productivity. A unit of capital in America delivers about half as much output again as an equivalent amount of spending in either Germany or Japan.

So a world-class company delivers on every front to its shareholders. It is financially sound but smart. It focuses on short-term performance but offers long-term value. It's a firm for all seasons.

Differentiation

The oral exam is about the seven attributes which a world-class company requires in order to meet the aforementioned financial goals. The first one that shareholders look for is differentiation or for a company to be unique in some way. Differentiation is the source of competitive advantage. You need clear blue water between yourself and your competitors. In the old days, you could conceal a hefty profit margin on a replicable, mediocre product from the competition. Nowadays, by way of the latest communication technologies, a million entrepreneurs can sniff out a market where excessive profits are being made easily and enter it themselves. No one is ever again going to make a lot of money by using the same machinery to produce the same thing and selling it to the same people as everybody else. It means you can either be small and dominate a local market, like Classical FM which Eon de Vos is establishing as a new radio station in South Africa; or you can be very large and dominate your niche worldwide. For anything intermediate in size, you have to be internationally competitive even if you are not dominant in your field. Should you try to be all things to all people, there's going to be pressure. Thus, national champions with copycat-able skills may become flabby also-rans when faced with lean and mean world-class competitors in the local race. Differentiation is also the reason why most mergers between world-class companies fail. Their cultures never gel. Alliances are more common now where each party retains its distinct identity.

13.4.1997 The best place to start when trying to explore the essence of a world-class company is to know who they are. So let's look at *Fortune's* annual list of America's most admired companies. The latest list which appeared on 3 March this year was headed by Coca-Cola (beverages). Then, in descending order, came Mirage Resorts (hotels, casinos and resorts); Merck (pharmaceuticals); United Parcel Service (mail, packaging and freight delivery); Microsoft (computer and data services); Johnson & Johnson (pharmaceuticals); Intel (electronics); Pfizer (pharmaceuticals); Procter & Gamble (soaps and cosmetics) and Berkshire Hathaway (diversified financial).

Further down the list but top in their respective industries were Shell Oil (petroleum); J.P. Morgan (banking); Merrill Lynch (broking); Boeing (aerospace); Chrysler (cars); Levi Strauss (apparel);

McDonald's (food retail); Campbell Soup (food); Freeport-McMoRan (mining); Gillette (metal products); Fluor (engineering); Caterpillar (industrial and farm equipment); Du Pont (chemicals); Kimberly-Clark (forest and paper products); Walt Disney (entertainment); Hewlett Packard (computers); Alcoa (metals) and 3M (scientific equipment).

How was the ranking done? *Fortune* sampled the opinions of 13 000 senior executives, outside directors and financial security analysts. They had to rate companies on eight key attributes: innovation; quality of management; value as a long-term investment; community and environmental responsibility; ability to attract, develop and keep talented people; quality of products or services; financial soundness and use of corporate assets. Coca-Cola was first in five categories including community and environmental responsibility and second in two others.

That's a great list of attributes for a world-class company. But right now I'd like to concentrate on one feature that is an underlying theme for all the companies mentioned above. The name of the game is differentiation – to be nongeneric or unique in some way. The reason is that in today's global contest any profit made out of generic or common features will be eroded to a minimum by competition. No more territorial rights or protective barriers exist for companies to hide behind. Thus, in order to maintain satisfactory margins, something about your business has to be very special, like an exclusive product, service, brand, corporate culture, group of employees, mining deposit, etc.

The ratio of Microsoft and Intel's headline earnings to gross turnover is 24 per cent and 22 per cent respectively. Coca-Cola's ratio is 17 per cent. By South African standards these are phenomenally high margins. Any company here basking in such good fortune would be considered vulnerable to competition. However, there's nothing else in the world like Windows 95, the Pentium chip and Coke. As one of a kind, they dominate their niches in a perfectly permissible way.

South African companies will need to follow the same principles of differentiation and specialisation. Any excessive profits made in the past out of being the national champion of a closed economy will now surely be at risk with the entry of America's most admired companies into our own market. To rise to the challenge, each of us will have to find something that sets our product or service, or just the way we do business, apart from the rest of the competition in the world. There's no room any more for companies which want to be average or similar to their peers. Those days are gone for good.

Branding

A powerful means of differentiation is branding. Most brands have a highly nationalistic element. Think about a tot of Scotch. What about greater emphasis on an African or even a South African brand? The Palace at the Lost City is a world-class facility that draws the foreign tourists precisely because it is designed to be an African experience.

27.4.1997 According to a new book, *The World's Greatest Brands,* compiled by leading international brand consultancy Interbrand, the top ten brands in order of rank are as follows: McDonald's, Coca-Cola, Disney, Kodak, Sony, Gillette, Mercedes Benz, Levis, Microsoft and Marlboro. Eight American, one Japanese and one German brand.

Each brand is assessed according to four criteria. The first is brand "weight" which is related to the dominance the brand exhibits in the market. For example, McDonald's is the leading brand in the quick-service restaurant industry. Second is brand "length" – the possibility the brand has for extending itself into other markets. Virgin's development from records into an airline, soft drinks and radio is cited as a prime instance of extension. Third is brand "breadth", a measure of the brand's popularity across age, religion, gender and nationality. Coke is an obvious choice in this category. Fourth is brand "depth" which is a gauge of customers' commitment to the brand. The Body Shop in the UK has a loyal following because of its devotion to environmental causes.

The list of top brands illustrates a key feature of world-class companies. You only join the club if you consistently offer value for money over a long period of time. There's a limit to the premium a brand can command. Philip Morris had to bow to this rule when, on 2 April 1993, they announced that they were lopping 40 cents off a pack of Marlboro cigarettes and saw their share price plunge by nearly one quarter. Only Microsoft is a relative newcomer to the list. Hence, the visionary leaders of world-class companies build organisational clocks that continue to tick well after they're gone. It takes years of patience and unwavering quality to earn a world-class reputation but those companies which do, tend to stay there. The list is amazingly stable.

In the 1960s, marketing experts were predicting a blander, more homogeneous world as companies and brands went global. Precisely the opposite has happened, as the list shows. Nothing could be more American than a McDonald's hamburger, a bottle of Coke or Levi jeans. Nothing displays Japanese genius for microelectronics like Sony or German engineering dependability like Mercedes. Rather than subduing national identity, world-class companies blatantly thrive and trade on it. It is their main means of differentiation. What could be more flamboyantly Italian than a red Ferrari or English-heritage-on-wheels than a Rolls Royce?

This provides a clue for what we have to do here if we want to enjoy a world-class premium for our products in the marketplace. We must exploit the one quality we possess which no American, European or Far Eastern company has: our location in Africa. We should therefore be using powerful African imagery to promote the products we sell overseas. Whether it's furniture; beer; wine; jewellery; drapery; clothing; films; music; whatever, we have to carve out a unique African niche. It sounds ambitious seeing that nobody has yet done it on a grand scale except in the tourist industry where it is obvious. Even here, cynics will say that TV scenes of Rwandan refugees reverberate far more in the Western consciousness than the sweeping plains of the Serengeti.

Be that as it may, the essence of being world class is not only being original but also having sufficient confidence in one's roots to use them at the core of any marketing strategy or advertising campaign. No other African country has the immediate potential to cash in on the "genuinely made in Africa" label like us because we have the most modern economy. There are perhaps ten million middle-class African-Americans plus many millions of other Americans – all with plenty of disposable income – who would be turned on by African themes. Let's satisfy them and thereby develop our own world-class brands.

Focus/Global player

The second and third attributes of a world-class company are focus and being a global player. It will be very difficult for a South African company of any size to meet the global norm of 5 × 10 × 10 in earnings per share growth and total return by adopting a defensive strategy on its own national turf. We will have to fight our foreign foes on theirs. But that means a change in mindset. It's no good any more having the philosophy that if it sells in Benoni, then that's all right. Moreover, Jack Welch of General Electric has shown that you can run a diversified business and win, providing there's focus in each business and a learning, sharing and action-driven culture encompassing all of them. Focus is a key message for South African management who, because of the shortage of expertise, have spread themselves very thin over a wide range of responsibilities. In an open economy, they can be taken to the cleaners by the focused professionals.

20.4.1997 Looking through the top ten most admired companies in America, one is struck by the focus they have. An exception is Berkshire Hathaway which is a diversified financial holding company with a stock-picking genius, Warren Buffett, as chairman. Otherwise, they are all involved in a single industry. In the case of Coca-Cola, the leader of the pack, we're really talking about a single product which hasn't changed since Dr John Pemberton's original syrup recipe in 1886. This goes to show that world-class management eat, breathe and sleep in narrow niches. They ensure that Jack of all trades remains master of none.

Even General Electric, placed eighteenth on the "admired" list and conventionally called a conglomerate, is really a stable of a dozen thoroughbreds. As chairman of GE – with incidentally the largest market capitalisation of any company in the US – Jack Welch has stated that each of his divisions has to be No. 1 or No. 2 in its respective global market. Otherwise, it has to be fixed, sold or closed. GE combines the benefits of a diversified portfolio of businesses with the need for dedicated management.

If you remember the book published in 1982 entitled *In Search of Excellence* by Tom Peters and Bob Waterman, one of the principles mentioned was "stick to the knitting", i.e. remain with the business

19

the company knows best. With the world turning into Marshall McLuhan's global village, the validity of this principle has intensified. However, there's one caveat: while the process of knitting doesn't change, the patterns do. In other words, companies should stay with their core competencies but adapt their range of products and services to the changing times. Plenty of highly focused businesses meet dismal fates because they don't see this distinction.

It may sound trite to say that world-class companies not only display focused excellence but also possess global reach. Hence, the term Coca-colonisation! Yet, many South African entrepreneurs have been strangely reticent to market abroad their products and services as and when they have developed them to world-class potential. Perhaps it's due to isolation during the years of apartheid or lack of confidence. But now sanctions have disappeared, our local businesses must break free. Given increasing competition on our home turf, the only way to grow our earnings per share at anything like world-class rates is to challenge the opposition on their own turf. You don't have to be present in their markets as long as your exports are in demand there. Hollywood proves that you can produce something locally that is marketable everywhere. All you need is a web site on the Internet.

To whet the appetite, there's a $20 trillion a year global market out there for the taking – 200 times larger than South Africa's. Fortunes can be made much quicker these days, but no one should be deceived into thinking of easy pickings. You need plenty of "chutzpah" to make it – the kind of can-do spirit epitomised by a T-shirt I came across in Jerusalem which said: "Don't worry America, Israel is behind you".

When Bill Gates visited South Africa recently, I heard that he arrived on a plane from India at 1 am. He got to the residence where he was staying in Johannesburg at 2 am. A few hours later, he gave a breakfast talk. Thereafter he answered questions impeccably not only on the future of the computer industry in the world at large, but on Microsoft's future role in Africa and South Africa down to the last detail. Despite constantly crossing different time zones to review his empire and being seriously rich at R200 billion, he never loses focus. That's world class for you!

Innovation

The fourth attribute of a world-class company is an innovative spirit to cope with the perpetual transition caused by accelerating technological change. As the tempo quickens, the champions will be the dancers who keep in time with the new beat. Of the top 100 companies in the US in 1917, only fifteen survive on the list today. The other 85 quit the ballroom floor, as products of the mind replaced those of the earth. It's all part of the "brain wave" replacing the "brawn wave".

1.6.1997 Of the current generation of scenario planners, Peter Schwartz of the Global Business Network in California stands out as a master of the art. He is responsible for the beautiful distinction between "lock-in" and "perpetual transition" industries.

A lock-in industry is one where technological standards change slowly. Horses were locked in as a means of transport for many centuries. People profited out of making saddles and stage coaches. Then along came cars. Now a hundred years later, entire communities and business networks are devoted to the internal combustion engine and ancillaries like tyres and petrol. In the recording industry, we had 78s up to the 1950s, then LPs and 45s and now CDs and cassettes. In a locked-in world, each technology is around for several decades if not for a century or more. It's a nice place to do business in.

However, an increasing number of industries are moving into perpetual transition which is a great deal more uncomfortable. Welcome to the world where technological change has never been swifter. The classic example is the computer business. When IBM invented the personal computer, it had no idea that this machine would utterly transform the market. Before the PC, IBM actually set the standard for the mainframe and decided how long that standard would endure. It was long enough for IBM to make a fortune out of each generation of its computers. But the PC put a stop to that. It not only ensured that nobody would ever have the same dominance again in computer manufacture as IBM did before the PC, it also shortened product life cycles to about six months. That's how long it takes for a competitor to come out with a new PC, one with a more powerful memory or a smarter microprocessor. As one engineer put it, we're talking dog years now, not human years.

Basically, in a perpetual transition industry you only have a "bubble of value" to exploit. You are therefore obliged to undertake a global marketing blitz for your product so that everybody has access to it before it goes stale – like a Hollywood movie. The only financial ratio that counts is the payback period: are you going to make more money out of the product in six months than all the money you've poured into it? Discounted cash flow yields over twenty years are obsolete because positive cash flows beyond the first year are doubtful. And finally you don't put lock-in managers in charge of perpetual transition businesses because they go bust. You need the guys with the ponytails!

Yet world-class companies survive this immense challenge through innovation and technological agility. These two attributes combine to give them the ability to launch wave after wave of new products and stay ahead of the field. Research and development programmes can be as high as 5 per cent of gross turnover in order to build up a sufficient reserve of fresh ideas or "invisible assets" as they're called. Andy Grove who is head of Intel, maker of the Pentium chip, has written a book called *Only the Paranoid Survive*. His theme is that you have to be obsessed about beating your competitors to the market all the time to be a success like Intel. Intel builds a $2 billion factory every year before it knows what product it's going to put through it.

The game of perpetual transition is one that a limited number of local companies comprehend. It demands a fleet-footedness that is normally reserved for small businesses and lots of "skunk-works" (internal task groups) dreaming up new inventions. Bell Labs in America is the mother of all skunk-works with the invention of the transistor and 26 000 other patents to its credit. Perpetual transition necessitates a managerial competence which can span numerous "bubbles of value" as opposed to a few long-term projects. Moreover, like a treadmill, the game never stops. And it doesn't just apply to high-tech industries either. The majority of commodities and manufactured products have experienced price declines in real terms during this century. Not because demand has diminished. Quite to the contrary, we've witnessed falling price booms as miners and manufacturers get smarter at producing things cheaper. Services are bound to follow. In these circumstances, the prize of highest margin goes to the company which through continual innovation can cut its unit costs the fastest.

Falling price boom

A falling price boom is becoming common in many industries. The idea, therefore, that the real prices of raw materials and engineered commodities (like cars and televisions) will improve in the long term is a mirage. It's the first guy on the block to develop a new technique who makes the most money. This does not mean that embarking on a savage cost-cutting drive is sensible. Indeed, it may well be that a substantial increase in expenditure on training can yield a lower unit cost if there is a more than compensating improvement in productivity. Contrariwise, a slash in training can actually raise unit costs. The other sensible strategy is to focus on speciality areas which take you out of the commodity rut. As somebody said, the only difference between a groove and a grave is depth!

29.6.1997 Gordon Moore, one of the founders of the microprocessor manufacturer Intel, formulated a law thirty years ago which has proved remarkably accurate. According to Moore's Law, the number of transistors on a silicon chip would double every eighteen months. This would lead to either of the following consequences: you'd get double the computing performance for the same price every eighteen months or you'd get the same computing performance for half the price.

For the thirty years since Moore put forward his law, technological innovation in the computer industry has indeed taken place at the dizzying pace he suggested. Thus, while demand for personal computers has grown exponentially around the world, a soaring performance-to-price ratio has meant that suppliers have stayed ahead of the game. Brian Reading, one of the consultants to Anglo's London scenario team, captured this trend with his phrase "falling price boom". Reading's phrase may not sound revolutionary, but it turns elementary economic theory on its head.

By definition, a boom say on the stock exchange or in the property market means a significant improvement in the general level of prices. If prices fall in either of these two sectors, calling it a boom would be a contradiction in terms. However, no one would dispute the fact that the personal computer business is booming and no one would deny that the price per unit of computing power or memory capacity has consistently fallen. The reversal in the chain of causation is responsible for this perplexing state of affairs. No longer is growing demand in the market driving prices up, which brings forth additional supply. Innovation is driving prices down, which leads to an expansion in demand. Opportunities multiply in a falling price boom in a way that they don't in a classical rising price boom. Thus along with the realistic possibility that one day every home will have a personal computer comes the scenario that every car will incorporate an appropriate computerised management system.

The reason this shift in economic paradigm is so crucial is that variations of Moore's Law are spreading like wildfire to other industries as well. *The Economist* ran an article recently on the death of distance. Ultimately, the cost of an international telephone call will decline towards zero on account of advances in telecommunication technology. People will pay a regular levy to be a member of a particular network and thereafter will be able to make as many telephone calls as they like to any location in the world absolutely free. This isn't a pipe dream. It could be reality before we move into the next century. The marginal cost to the telephone company of each call, whatever the distance, is already minute.

Moreover, the membership levies necessary to recover all overhead costs including the installation and maintenance of the physical network will themselves fall as competition between world-class companies leads to greater efficiencies. We're in a borderless world where national telecom monopolies will simply disappear and the consumer will benefit mightily. The Internet as I write offers a method of making international calls at local rates (providing you've got the right voice transmission equipment).

In the multimedia field generally, a recently enunciated law is that bandwidth is set to treble every twelve months. This implies even more bewildering change than with microprocessors. TVs will become PCs, video telephones will be commonplace and the information superhighway will triple its number of lanes every year, speeding up the Internet in the process. As the saying goes, you ain't seen nothing yet!

Sensitive radar system

The fifth attribute of a world-class company is a sensitive radar system to detect unexpected futures. The reason the Rothschilds became the world's most famous banking family in the last century was that their intelligence network was more efficient than their competitors. Their agents rode faster horses to deliver major news flashes to their bosses, who were then ahead of the market. In addition, the more you focus, the more you must be prepared to alter course if your assumptions about the future prove incorrect. It doesn't matter how brilliant your management is, there is nothing they can do if your line is going out of fashion. It is equally important that, having identified the blip on the screen, you know what you can and cannot change so that you can focus on the one and adapt to the other. Moreover, you should also distinguish between what you should and shouldn't change about your business. Change for change's sake can be dangerous because it takes years to build up a brand and corporate image.

6.7.1997 There's a shopping mall in the northern suburbs of Johannesburg that used to remind me of Alfred Hitchcock's thriller *The Birds*. In the evening, the mall was so solidly packed with teeny-boppers twittering amongst themselves that the noise and the numbers felt positively threatening. It was hard to thread one's way between the throng to a restaurant, let alone a cinema. But the place today reminds one of a silent mausoleum. Like a flock of starlings, the young have migrated to another "in" spot. One minute they're here, next minute they're gone.

The market's like that. Unexpected discontinuities abound. To be a world-class business, therefore, you need a sensitive radar system which is permanently switched on and the ability to turn on a dime. No strategy is sacrosanct. Every decision is subject to change. When Microsoft picked up on its radar screen that the Internet was going to be a lot more powerful and universal than it had previously anticipated, it immediately cancelled its plan for constructing its own Net. Instead, it put all its resources behind providing software to enable easier access to the Internet and make it a more powerful tool for the user. Quite an extraordinary U-turn for such a large and successful company when bigness and success normally blind you.

Jack Welch who runs General Electric has no illusions about the uncertainty of doing business in the modern world. If a company goes bad on him, a directive is immediately issued to management to fix it, sell it or close it. No romantic attachment, no extended turnaround is allowed to magnify the losses and play havoc with the economic value-added ratio. He acts with the swiftness of a small entrepreneur with a lean bank balance. Dogs are put down or transformed back into stars.

It may sound strange that having talked about focus and dedication as prime qualities of world-class companies, I now stress open-mindedness and flexibility. But life is never simple. Logically, the more focused a business becomes, the quicker its leadership must sense when it's going up a blind alley and respond. The change required may be small – an amendment to the product or service line-up in the same industry. But occasionally it behoves a complete metamorphosis of the company over time, an example being Minnesota Mining and Manufacturing, or 3M as we call it nowadays. It evolved from a mine in 1902 to sandpaper to Scotch tape to a diversified group involved in technologies embracing electronics, information, graphic arts, photographic films, adhesive tapes and health care. And it did all this while keeping its world-class competency intact.

Sometimes, the decision to change is wrong and you have to reverse yourself. Coca-Cola had that experience when it introduced New Coke, but soon realised that tampering with the brand was the last thing that people wanted. Management didn't pause when they spotted the error. They rectified it immediately and learnt a whole new set of ways of marketing the original product. They're flying now.

I remember reading Barbara Tuchman's *The March of Folly*. She investigated why history was replete with examples of politicians and generals doggedly pursuing policies contrary to their self-interest – how the Renaissance popes provoked the Protestant secession, how the British lost America and America betrayed herself in Vietnam. The answer common to all of them was folly brought about by conceit and by the refusal to lose face. No alternatives were foreseen or considered. Flexibility, though, should not be mistaken for ambivalence. If, in 1297, the Scottish hero William Wallace had said to his forces before the battle of Stirling, "Gentlemen, we have two scenarios – victory or defeat", he wouldn't have won it. Once committed, be decisive.

Business is the same as war when it comes to obstinacy. Punishment is swift and harsh as nemesis follows hubris. The constant worry of Andy Grove and Bill Gates, the two shining lights of the computer business, is that a fifteen-year-old genius may be beavering away in some garage on some revolutionary product which will consign them to the dole queue. Humility is their armour. They never relent, they are the opposite of complacent. Now you know why the meek really do inherit the earth.

Wrong predictions

Here are some examples of how wrong our predictions can be. This is the reason why we must paint alternative and often uncomfortable scenarios which can test the latent assumptions of a company's "official future". Often a strategic plan is merely a reflection of the CEO's desired future, because the messenger doesn't want to get killed. But there's no point in having the troops march in one direction when the actual future is taking another. Someone asked me the other day what the role of a scenario planner was. I replied that it was akin to the court jester of old who sold unpalatable futures to the king, using humour to minimise the risk of being beheaded! To show how improbable the future really is, imagine writing the correct scenario for twentieth-century Germany a hundred years ago. The country will fight two world wars, lose them both, suffer hyperinflation in between the wars, be split into two after the second one, reunite and emerge as the dominant economic power in Europe.

13.7.1997 A week ago, I dwelt upon how important it is to acknowledge our inability to forecast the future. Hands up all those who foresaw the vertiginous descent in the gold price the following day. Not me – it took my breath away. We need the antennae of the wiliest insect to sense what lies ahead. To drive the point home, I would like to mention some of the wrong predictions made by eminent people in recent history which have turned out to be embarrassing howlers. The list of quotations is taken from an article in *Newsweek* entitled "Cloudy Days in Tomorrowland". In a recent video that I did on scenario methodology called *Beyond Plan B*, I described how Western Union turned down the patent for the telephone when offered it by

Alexander Graham Bell for a paltry $100 000 in 1876. The president of Western Union at the time, William Orton, said: "What use could this company make of an electrical toy?"

In retrospect, the lack of appreciation for some blockbuster inventions appears remarkable. In 1897, Lord Kelvin, a Scottish mathematician, physicist and former president of the Royal Society, surmised: "Radio has no future." Two years later, Charles H. Duell, the then US Commissioner of Patents, made the observation: "Everything that can be invented, has been invented." This was followed in 1901 by H.G. Wells's remark: "I must confess that my imagination refuses to see any sort of submarine doing anything but suffocating its crew and floundering at sea." Concerning transport on land, a president of the Michigan Savings Bank gave the following advice to Horace Rackham, Henry Ford's lawyer, when trying to dissuade him from investing in the Ford Motor Company in 1903: "The horse is here to stay, but the automobile is only a novelty – a fad." Fortunately, Rackham ignored the advice, bought $5 000 worth of stock and sold it several years later for $12,5 million.

Above the ground, Wilbur Wright, the US aviation pioneer, made the following admission in 1908: "I must confess that in 1901, I said to my brother, Orville, that man will not fly for fifty years. Ever since, I have distrusted myself and avoided all predictions." In the same vein, Marshall Ferdinand Foch, French military strategist and future World War I commander, said in 1911: "Airplanes are interesting toys, but of no military value." After that war, Josephus Daniels, former US secretary of the navy, made this prediction in 1922: "Nobody now fears that a Japanese fleet could deal an unexpected blow on our Pacific possessions. Radio makes surprise impossible." I wonder if he was still living at the time of Pearl Harbour! Nearly as bad was David Lloyd George's comment in 1934: "Believe me, Germany is unable to wage war."

Seven years earlier, in 1927, Harry Warner of Warner Brothers asked the question: "Who the hell wants to hear actors talk?" But even when the world moved on from silent movies, Darryl F. Zanuck, head of 20th Century-Fox said in 1946: "Television won't be able to hold on to any market it captures after the first six months. People will soon get tired of staring at a plywood box every night." Elsewhere in the world of entertainment, Decca Records in 1962 wrote the ultimate rejection note: "We don't like their sound. Groups of guitars are on the way out." They were talking about the Beatles.

Another great invention of modern times is the computer. It elicited this opinion from the journal, *Popular Mechanics,* in 1949: "Computers in the future may perhaps only weigh 1,5 tons." In 1977, Kenneth Olsen who founded Digital Equipment mused: "There is no reason for any individual to have a computer for their home."

In the topsy-turvy field of stocks and shares, an American statistician called Roger Babson said towards the end of 1928: "The election of Hoover should result in continued prosperity for 1929." Irving Fisher, professor of economics at Yale University, remarked in 1929 itself: "Stocks have reached what looks like a permanently high plateau." Presumably, they were both victims of the Crash. In a moment of denial, Joseph Kennedy claimed in 1936: "I have no political ambitions for myself or my children." Finally, the quickest contradiction of a prophecy happened to an unnamed general in the American Civil War who erroneously harangued his troops with the words: "Don't worry. The enemy is too far away for any of us to be sh . . ." I rest my case.

Ability to attract talented young people

The sixth attribute of a world-class company is the ability to attract talented young people. Share options are as good a way as any since they have the capacity to give hotshots a high net worth before they're thirty. Salary increases, on the other hand, are usually neutralised by the rising spending habits of one's spouse and family.

20.7.1997 Probably the most important attribute of a world-class company is the ability to attract, develop and keep TYPs – talented young people – so that they turn into TOPs or talented old people. Ultimately the quality of a company rests on the quality of its management and employees. In the short run, you might strike it lucky with a product that has mass appeal or a discovery of a mineral bonanza. But over the long haul, your edge is your people – the smile on the face of the bank teller, the warmth in the greeting of the receptionist. As one wise person put it: "To be world class, you have to treat your people as an asset on the balance sheet rather than a cost on your profit and loss account." Thus, the human resource function has come to occupy centre stage.

Large companies with generous bursary schemes have no problem attracting intelligent students. They put them through tertiary education and get them started in their business careers. The trouble occurs later on when the new recruits have worked off their loans and want to spread their wings by taking on genuine responsibilities. If the development phase isn't followed quickly by the real thing, companies are vulnerable to having their best and brightest poached by unscrupulous competitors who are prepared to piggyback in a parasitic way on the training programmes of others. The latter can inflate their offers to ridiculous levels as they have no training costs to write off. Everywhere in the world, the up-and-coming join this lucrative merry-go-round. Thus, the key issue in relation to talented people is retention, not recruitment.

The other threat in the postmodernist society that we live in is that the younger generation is more individualistic than their forebears. They become more quickly frustrated with bureaucracy. They want the space to be entrepreneurs. They are inclined to leave organisations which don't grant them the extra degrees of freedom they expect. They are more confident of pursuing their own interests if need be. Silicon Valley in California is full of stories of hi-tech geniuses leaving the established firms to set up their own businesses in garages or attics. Venture capital is plentiful and the wonders of modern communication permit any inventor of a "killer application" to join the get-incredibly-rich-quick crowd relatively easily.

So what does a world-class company do? First and foremost it creates an environment in which the high flyers are never bored. They are fast-tracked. They come into regular contact with top management. There is no climate of fear to cow them. On the contrary, they are expected to speak their minds and their ideas are given serious consideration. They receive regular feedback on their performance and merit is significantly rewarded. No equal misery for all! They become captains of small yachts early on in their careers in order to learn the nuts and bolts of steering a business into the future; how power should be wielded to mould the crew into a successful team and when to change course when circumstances dictate. Later on the boats get bigger and the voyages more complex.

Another major difference these days is the granting of a genuine stake in the business, usually by the way of share options, virtually straightaway. Incentive schemes are no longer confined to the board and senior management. They reach all the way down. For example, a visit to Coca-Cola's web site reveals the following management philosophy: "Since our directors, officers and employees own more than 15% of the outstanding shares of the Company, our corporate objective is clearly aligned with that of our external share owners." Quite so. Of course, the great feature of joining a world-class company is that such schemes have a very high probability of giving a young employee real wealth down the line. On the assumption that a company is providing a 20 per cent per annum real return to its shareholders, the shares under option double in value every four years. The disposable income of even the yuppiest family doesn't quite rise at that rate so there's money to be put away for a rainy day.

It is not surprising that relatively few senior positions in world-class companies are filled by outsiders. They have, through jealously guarding their talent, ensured that for every top guy a bevy of able young successors are available. That way you burn the eternal flame. You don't die like the average company after forty years. My old school, Winchester College, celebrated its 615th anniversary this year. I trust Coca-Cola will do the same in 2501 A.D.

Social and environmental responsibility

The seventh attribute of a world-class company is to be socially and environmentally responsible. Many governments are girding themselves up to stamp out "corruption eruption". The OECD has agreed to formulate a treaty making it illegal for firms from member countries to bribe foreign officials. The World Bank is considering a "blacklist" of companies suspected of corruption. In future, nothing will make a company lose its world-class badge faster than being exposed for greasing palms, unfair labour practices or insensitivity to the environment. In the 90s green – not greed – is good.

27.7.1997 The newest prerequisite for a company to qualify as world class is one that is often written off as soft by line management (in contrast to the hard issues of costs and production). It is the matter of social and environmental responsibility. This requirement has seriously grown in importance – as several large companies have painfully discovered lately.

Shell had to cope with the controversies over its activities in Nigeria and the disposal of the Brent Spar oil rig. The fall-out prompted Cor Herkstroter, the Chairman of the Dutch half of Shell, to admit that multinationals like his are being haunted by "a ghost in the system – some sort of slight blurring that causes us to make subtle, but in the end far-reaching, mistakes in assessing developments". It also spurred the company to include a commitment to human rights and sustainable development in its new statement of business principles. Not all shareholders are pacified. They want an external review body to monitor progress against the principles and a director to be held personally accountable for the company's performance.

BP's last annual general meeting was dominated by a debate over its shift towards politically and environmentally sensitive areas from which it will source part of its oil and gas production. Rio Tinto has had a similar experience vis-à-vis its future mining plans. US tobacco companies have reached a provisional deal with plaintiffs that could entail a pay-out worth $368,5 billion over 25 years into a smokers' compensation fund. Anti-abortion activists in America, by urging consumers to boycott Hoechst, the German pharmaceuticals company, have compelled the company to end its involvement with RU 486 – the controversial abortion pill. Meanwhile, Swiss banks are accused of holding gold plundered by Hitler's Nazis.

And so the pressure mounts. Yet it is not just the highly focused NGOs like Greenpeace who act as watchdogs. The sheer pervasiveness and power of the media ensure that every world-class company from now on will have to obey internationally acceptable social and environmental norms in the course of their activities. We're in a post-CNN world where all things need to be frontstage and transparent. You'll simply be struck off the "world class" list if covert tricks in some backwater are exposed.

The other day, on a TV programme beamed to millions around the world, a young interviewer held up the new model of a running shoe. She said to the CEO of the company that designed the shoe: "You must be proud of this. Note the sophisticated heel cushioning and torsion bar in the centre of the sole to minimise ankle twist." "Indeed, I am, ma'am," was his reply. "Well," she exclaimed with an angelic look, "did you know that this actual shoe was produced by a twelve-year-old boy in Bangladesh working twelve-hour days seven days a week for $3 a month?" Game, set and match to her. No sweat shops permitted.

You have to be a company that people believe in. Marks and Spencer, the founders of one of Britain's premier retailers, both took that principle very seriously. Be decent to your employees and they'll be decent back to you. Do the opposite once and years of carefully cultivating the corporate image go up in smoke. A generous and honourable spirit is as important as the talent to make a buck. Think of a thirty-minute in-depth interview on CNN with one of their ace reporters. Will the CEO pass the test with a clean slate on every aspect of the business?

Hence, it's not just the unions and labour legislation which are making companies behave better. The market has joined in as well. To do good business, you have to be good in business. In the short term, the biggest change for South African companies could well be the way annual general meetings are run. We're bound to fall in line with the more probing approach adopted overseas as activists seek a larger role in corporate affairs. It'll keep us on our toes to be a just employer and custodian of the environment. Time to listen and learn!

Striking a balance

As with everything else a balance is required between economic development and the conservation of the environment. World class means striking the right compromise. On the one hand we don't want to live in Waterworld *as a result of global warming, but on the other hand we do want to raise people's standard of living.*

3.9.1995 Greenpeace made headlines recently when they managed to get Shell to reverse its decision to dump the Brent Spar, a huge oil-storage platform, in the deep North Atlantic. It is now going to be towed to shore and broken up on land. Reputable scientists argue that this second option carries greater environmental risks than the first one.

Whatever the truth of the matter, these headline-grabbing events tend to distort the environmental debate. In the public mind, it comes across as industry in the one corner versus the environment in the other. We have had our own controversies here such as the proposal to mine mineral sands close to St Lucia in Natal or to put up a new steelworks at Saldanha Bay. Each time, a powerful environmental lobby produces persuasive reasons as to why an increase in economic activity should be sacrificed in the interests of environmental preservation. Their case may be valid but emotion runs so high that the facts get obscured. Seldom does your average citizen receive an objective list of pros and cons on which a rational decision can be made.

As with all things, a balance has to be struck between economic development and environmental health. To argue that the two are mutually exclusive goals and the pursuit of one has to be at the expense of the other is absurd. In fact, without economic development the environment cannot be preserved. It is such a shame that this simple fact is not acknowledged by the green movements. Demonising business as the only threat to the environment is the easy way out, designed to get lots of applause from the nonbusiness sector. But antipollution measures and other actions to minimise the impact of humanity on nature are always expensive. If South Africa wants to apply high standards to keep the environment clean, then the country will have to transform itself into a healthy economy that can afford those standards.

I find it interesting that some environmentalists talk passionately of adopting a holistic approach towards life while others do exactly the opposite by rejecting all but the environmental perspective. Perhaps students doing environmental studies at university should be obliged to do some business courses so that they can at least see where the other side is coming from when conflicts over the environment arise. The reverse should obviously apply to business students who need a bit of environmental acumen. Then debates between the two groups will not deteriorate into slanging matches.

In the book *South African Environments into the 21st Century* which Brian Huntley, Roy Siegfried and I wrote together, we posed three scenarios which are still relevant to South Africa's future. "Paradise Lost" was the really pessimistic one where the infrastructure of the country collapses because of a breakdown of law and order and negative economic growth. Deforestation and general plunder of natural resources follow, which means that our "world in one country" is reduced to a desolate wasteland.

The second scenario was "Boom and Bust" where we tread the path taken by the Asian tigers with scant regard for the environment. With total emphasis on industrial and commercial expansion, we have an economic boom followed by an environmental bust.

The third scenario was "Rich Heritage". Under this scenario, a robust economy and a politically stable community provide the means and the commitment required for the wise use of natural resources. Pressure on the latter is reduced by more efficient resource management systems and technologies. South Africa joins the ranks of newly industrialised countries with full knowledge of the hazards and costs of imprudent exploitation of the environment. It is this last scenario that we should all aim for in the long run and not be distracted by fleeting controversies that pit business against the environment.

World-class agriculture
Given South Africa's fragile ecology, farmers especially have to exercise self-restraint whilst turning a profit. Sustainable development is an essential feature of world-class agriculture.

18.12.1994 The Restitution of Land Rights Act has turned out to be a model piece of legislation. Justice and pragmatism have been balanced with much care and ingenuity. The drafters are to be congratulated. Nevertheless, implementation faces some daunting economic and environmental realities.

Starting with the economic picture, farming has to be one of the toughest businesses around. In the last century, the majority of Americans were employed in agriculture. That figure has now reduced to 3 per cent not because the other 97 per cent have in the meantime been forcibly removed from the land, but because the manufacturing and service sectors have proved to be more attractive alternatives for earning a living. Similar though less dramatic falls in agricultural employment have been evident in Europe and Japan.

35

Through better fertilisers, irrigation and the introduction of improved plant and animal species by hybridisation, cross-breeding and latterly genetic engineering, agricultural yields have shot up. Thus continual surpluses of meat, dairy products, grain and wine have been created by improved technology. Farms have been merged into ever larger agri-businesses to obtain the economies of scale necessary to compete in world markets. Moreover, governments have striven to keep their national agricultural sectors afloat with enormous subsidies to the farmers (currently estimated to be between $200 and $300 billion annually in developed countries).

South Africa has not escaped these trends. The intricate system of marketing boards and subsidies has to a certain extent shielded farmers from the worst of the fluctuations in world agricultural prices. Nevertheless, the present level of farmers' debt bears witness to the rigours and uncertainties of a life dedicated to the land.

But what makes the farmers here the ultimate entrepreneurs is the environmental challenges. Consider these statistics. The total area of South Africa is 122 million hectares of which just under 101 million hectares are farmland. Of this only 17 million hectares are considered arable because of adequate rainfall. The remaining 84 million hectares of nonarable farmland are natural vegetation, used primarily for grazing. With under 14 per cent of its land surface being arable, South Africa is categorised as an arid country. About 27 per cent of the country is drought-stricken for more than 50 per cent of the time.

Yet when the floods come – as they regularly do – they inflict heavy damage in terms of lives lost, property swept away and the vanishing of topsoil. Annually, South Africa flushes some 300 to 400 million tons of topsoil down its rivers. If this soil was stolen from this country and loaded onto seven-ton trucks, then bumper to bumper they would extend seven and a half times around the circumference of the globe. The mean rate of soil loss of around three tons per hectare per year compares with a mean rate of soil formation of 0,1 tons. So the average farm is losing soil at thirty times the rate that it is being created.

Apart from having to face the hardship of climate, farmers have the problem of cattle and goats turning grassland into desert. In particular, cattle are incredibly inefficient at converting grass and water into protein compared to local game. They literally devour the environment. Locusts, invasive plants like jointed cactus, encroachment on the veld by urbanisation, roads and industry, water shortages caused by rivers drying up and by dams silting up – the farmers have to cope with all these factors and still turn a profit.

I am in no way implying that any of the foregoing difficulties should slow down the process of land restitution. However, it would be imprudent to ignore the fact that land in itself is not an asset. It is only an asset because of the productive and profitable use to which it can be put by the owner. Accompanying any restitution, therefore, must be training where necessary – not only in appropriate farming methods but also in entrepreneurship and business administration. An awareness of exactly how much the local environment can sustain in either crop or livestock production has to be instilled. Restitution therefore involves the transfer of knowledge and land at the same time.

Scarce water
Water in the long run is a scarce resource in South Africa despite the recent good rains. The provision of clean water to impoverished communities should top the list of any corporate outreach programme.

22.1.1995 When water is in plentiful supply, it is something everyone takes for granted. In fact, being a relatively cheap commodity, it is often wasted. It is only when water is rationed or even cut off that people suddenly realise how dependent they are on it for every aspect of their life. No longer is a regular bath or shower feasible. Neither the dishes nor the clothes can be washed. Toilets can't be flushed. Most crucially, a casual drink can't be taken from the tap. So the fridge gets raided for what's bottled. When the fridge is empty, a trip is made to the local café to restock. But what happens when the café is empty and there's no water in town?

This adds up to a pretty scary scenario. But I paint it because Gauteng for example is one of the largest conurbations of human beings on this earth situated away from a major natural water source. Alas, it just so happens that where the gold was, the water isn't. Gauteng is kept alive by an ingenious network of dams and rivers piping the water from the south.

But the availability of water to the country as a whole is poor too. The total annual runoff of South Africa's rivers amounts normally to about 53 500 million cubic metres. On a per capita basis, this is but 19 per cent of the global average. Moreover, in some areas rivers can have ten consecutive years of less than average flow. El Nino – the condition that draws tropical rainfall eastwards to the Pacific Ocean's central region away from southern Africa – is not a new phenomenon. It is merely a recently discovered cause of a variability in rainfall that has always existed. Because of this variability and the high evaporation losses from storage in dams, it is estimated that only 62 per cent of the mean annual runoff of South Africa's rivers can be exploited economically.

Existing major dams in South Africa have a total capacity equivalent to 50 per cent of the total mean annual runoff. Virtually the entire runoff from the interior plateau is already captured. Luckily, with the commissioning of the R4 billion Lesotho Highlands Water Scheme and the careful management of existing supplies, Gauteng at least will make it through to the next century.

Currently, South Africa's population is around 40 million. To this figure, we are adding a million more thirsty mouths each year. The point is that water, not land, is ultimately what will determine how many inhabitants this country can sustain. Already, consumption of water in some rural areas is down to 9 litres per person per day, compared with the World Health Organisation's goal of 50 litres. In middle-class homes, two or three taps per resident is not unusual. In the Eastern Transvaal, there are places where there is one tap for no fewer than 760 people.

Yet it's not only quantity but also the quality of water that is crucial for life – or death. At present, an unacceptably high number of young children in rural areas die from diseases caused by contaminated water. Ask any rural community what their top priority is and they will say a supply of clean, potable water.

So what can be done? The digging of more boreholes where underground water exists is essentially a short-term measure. Supplies are not limitless and should really only be used as a top-up in emergencies. Building more dams in South Africa is more of a replacement strategy than one to expand supplies. Exotic answers like towing icebergs from Antarctica or removing the salt from sea water are incredibly expensive.

Cloud seeding to increase precipitation is unproven. Building a pipe line to draw from the Zambezi is not only dependent on Zimbabwe's approval but again is very costly.

It therefore comes down to water conservation and recycling. Half of South Africa's developed water resources goes to irrigation. Many irrigation schemes are heavily subsidised. Charging irrigation customers a more market-related price for water would diminish the number of really cost-inefficient schemes, allowing the water they consume to be diverted to more productive uses elsewhere. On a broader front, agriculture and industry need to concentrate even more on optimising production per litre of water consumed. This they will do anyway as water as a resource becomes scarcer and the price rises. As far as the recycling of water is concerned, technologies to do so are improving all the time. Plenty of opportunities still exist to be exploited in this field.

Hence, one must not be overly pessimistic. On the other hand, one must not hope that good times will be here again when this cycle of El Nino is over. Foresight and action are required.

Animal rights

Animal rights are becoming more generally acknowledged. Consumers will increasingly ask world-class food companies for evidence of the humane treatment of animals before they purchase meat, poultry, eggs, etc.

10.9.1995　Animal rights. Not so long ago, the phrase conjured up an image of slightly dotty old ladies who overspoil their pets and decide to leave their money to the local dog's home. Or of activists laying false trails for the hounds of the fox hunters. But in the UK right now, there are plenty of ordinary and very sane middle-class citizens who believe passionately that animals do have some form of rights. Indeed an August issue of *The Economist* devoted a section to "People and Animals".

The immediate cause of the widening controversy is the shipment of live animals – calves and lambs – from Britain to Europe. Demonstrations have been a daily occurrence in those seaside ports whence the animals are shipped. The demonstrators have looked anything but bohemian and anarchic. Most are middle-aged and respectable.

The Economist article quotes Wendy Bragg, a 52-year-old owner of a small bed-and-breakfast in Brightlingsea as follows: "I can't bear animals suffering. I can't bear anyone suffering. They've got no one to stand up for them except us. No one else will stop this evil trade – and it is an evil trade."

It might be argued that the British have always had a soft spot for animals. After all, the Royal Society for the Prevention of Cruelty to Animals was founded in 1824, some fifty years ahead of the National Society for the Prevention of Cruelty to Children. Yet one detects a long-term shift in values on what constitutes inconsiderate behaviour towards animals. This applies not only in Britain, but also in America, where there is a considerably higher proportion of vegetarians among teenagers than in previous generations. They refer to the meat section of a supermarket as a graveyard! No longer is the realm of being unreasonably cruel confined to trapping animals for furs, chasing them to exhaustion for recreation or using them as if they were inanimate objects in laboratory experiments. The whole chain of keeping animals on a farm, transporting them and slaughtering them is coming under a critical spotlight as well.

There are probably three reasons for this. First, the sheer scale of the meat, poultry and egg markets plus their competitiveness have driven the businesses involved to adopt factory-like practices that appear inhumane. Keeping chickens in battery cages and debeaking them are examples. Second, the 1990s are a "kinder" era where cruelty of any kind is more universally deplored. It is virtually impossible to buy an old-fashioned mousetrap in England anymore. Third, activists have very effectively used videos to show people footage of unnecessarily cruel acts towards animals and some of the more stomach-churning steps that turn the animal into a meal on the table. These revelations have literally put some of the more sensitive members of the community off their food when it is meat: they have become vegetarians. They are also inducing an increasing number of consumers to pay a premium for meat products or eggs which guarantee that certain standards of humaneness have been met. These standards are monitored by respected private organisations.

I can already hear the regular steak-eaters who read this article chuckling and saying that it will never happen in South Africa. We are too carnivorous. Like lions, we have no problem with meat. But changes in Western habits have a funny way of fetching up on our shores – particularly amongst the young. We have had the liberation struggle for humans. Who knows – the one for animals may be about to begin.

Return of the whale

The return of the whale is an example of the reward to mankind when nature is respected. It is heartening to hear that whales are to remain an endangered species out of range of the harpoons.

6.10.1996 Thar she blows! That was the cry from the old whaleboats as one of the crew spotted the prey and let fly a deadly harpoon at an unmissable target. For the first time in my life, I could use those words too. I've never seen a whale at close quarters before. But there she was with her calf close to the rocks at Sunnycove which is just out of Fish Hoek on the road to Simon's Town. She looked like a nuclear submarine. Although I couldn't make out her full length, I'm told the average is 14 metres – or ten elephants in a row. At over 40 tons, she wouldn't win a weight-watchers' competition.

She was a Southern Right whale who had come all the way from the Antarctic to have her baby in the relative shelter of False Bay with its gently sloping sandy bottom. Others go to calve off the southern coasts of Australia, New Zealand and South America. Later in the week, I saw many more whales breaching, lobtailing, spyhopping and sailing in the bay. The most impressive motion is breaching where they jump clean out of the water like a salmon or a trout. The only difference is that whales flip backwards, their tail flukes smacking the water with a mighty splash. It's a 40-ton reverse somersault!

This magnificent creature, notable for the white callosities which stand out like barnicles on the head, was almost hunted to extinction between 1790 and 1825. Over 12 000 whales were killed during that period. The name "Southern Right" denoted the fact that they were the "right" whales to catch. They were slow enough for the rowing boats, they floated when they were dead and they yielded a range of highly profitable meat, bone and oil products.

In 1935, they became a protected species. Now the worldwide pop-

41

ulation has returned to around 5 000 and is increasing by 7 per cent a year. The lifespan of a Southern Right is thought to exceed 50 years.

Coincidental with my first encounter with a whale, I attended the opening of the new conservatory at Kirstenbosch. There I met Sir Ghillean Prance who is Director of Kew Gardens in London, the equivalent of being the Chief Botanist of the Cosmos. Over tea in the restaurant in the Gardens, he explained that the world was now experiencing the Sixth Extinction – a period when many species are suddenly lost. For instance, the previous Extinction involved the disappearance of the dinosaurs. The current Extinction, he said, was the biggest and most widespread of them all with at least ten species vanishing forever each day. Unfortunately, the flora and fauna being lost did not have the same high visibility of the whales, although their function in the environment could be as critical. The sadness was that we would never know the potential value of many extinct species because they hadn't been discovered before they disappeared.

The Sixth Extinction is not altogether surprising given that one species – the human race – has multiplied by a factor of 10 in the last 300 years. With $5\frac{1}{2}$ billion of us, it means less space for the other species. Can't we learn from the inspirational example of the revival of the whales that, with care, there is still a place under the sun for every creature great and small? And remember – whales are good for tourism too.

Patrons of the arts

Besides being environmentally aware, world-class companies should also be patrons of the arts. The Medicis set a good example. A definitive measurement of the degree to which a company is socially responsible is the percentage of its dividends which it gives away to charity. One per cent is a minimum. Broadway needs a Wall Street to support it.

11.12.1994 "If one draws up a list of the greatest names associated with any country's history, as likely as not a name will be included from the arts. For Italy it might be Leonardo da Vinci, for England William Shakespeare, for Germany Ludwig van Beethoven." The quote came from John Kani, himself an actor of repute whose name would fittingly be mentioned in any roll call of illustrious South Africans. The occasion was a recent breakfast in aid of a trust to develop South African arts and culture across as wide a spectrum as possible.

The timing of the remark is perfect since the outlook for the future financing of the arts in this country looks increasingly uncertain. Government support for the arts is now vying with the other pressing needs of the RDP (Reconstruction and Development Programme). Private-sector donations to the arts have been under pressure for some time, partially because of general economic conditions, partially because business is also being asked to contribute towards education, health and other noble causes and finally because the arts can never compete with sport in terms of exposure gained from sponsorship.

On top of this, the market for local works of art in South Africa is limited. This reflects not only the modest total of disposable income available for artistic products, but also the fact that much of that income is being diverted into tickets to watch Hollywood movies and purchases of international books, CDs and tapes. An unfortunate consequence is that local art of an entirely original nature often fails to get off the ground because artists are compelled to stay in the mainstream to make a living. Moreover, a lot of the big spenders (such as companies) are conservative and want nothing more than a painting of cattle in the veld under storm-laden skies. The real tragedy, though, is that the remuneration of South Africa's top authors, painters, playwrights, actors, musicians, etc. is decidedly low by world standards – apart from the odd individual who has successfully broken into the international market.

I am in no way suggesting that we should go in for wholesale protectionism to force people to absorb local culture and in the process drive up prices of domestic art. Insistence on excessive local content is as dangerous in the artistic field as it is in industry, since it cuts people off from the global pool of new ideas. What one does want to see is a return to the old-fashioned system of patronage of up-and-coming artists. All three of the artistic superstars mentioned by John Kani lived off a combination of patronage and commissions for their work. The idea that a Renaissance artist lay on his back on suspended wooden planks painting chapel ceilings for inspiration and no material reward is enchanting, but false.

The first major patrons were the churches and the monarchs, but the Medicis changed all that. This Florentine family, having made a fortune out of banking and commerce, backed a number of the Italian Renaissance artists, including da Vinci, Michelangelo and Botticelli. Shakespeare was supported by the Earl of Southampton for whom, in return, he wrote several sonnets. Of Beethoven it was said that "he benefited from the patronage of aristocratic enthusiasts – this in spite of his uncouth manners, unattractive appearance, eccentric habits and ungovernable temper".

Today, rich individuals and institutions tend to support museums and galleries and buy the works of Old Masters. They do not offer, at least on the same scale as their predecessors, patronage or decent commissions to living artists. This is where trusts of the type launched by John Kani can play an invaluable role in the future of South African art. Obviously, the trustees must be a mixture of the artists themselves and those representing the funders.

As a professional musician of eight years' standing – from the age of fifteen to twenty-two – I can only but repeat the immortal words of Chuck Berry: "Go Johnny, Go, Go, Go." Raise lots of money.

The fight against AIDS
And the private sector should go flat out to help the government stop the spread of AIDS. It's all part of the seventh attribute of being world class. It is quite possible to stabilise and even curb the spread of the virus. Uganda, as one of the first African countries to face up to the problem, has shown the way. HIV prevalence rates among pregnant women dropped from 30 per cent in 1992 to 18 per cent in 1995. It's never over till the fat lady sings.

23.3.1997 Her eyes were jet black which contrasted with her straw-blonde hair. Her complexion reminded one of smooth porcelain while her vivacious features had inner strength and outer beauty. She spoke articulately with a faint Afrikaans accent. I guess she must have been around twenty years old. I never got her name from the TV programme covering Virodene and AIDS. But she danced for the camera with all the graceful energy and lithe movements of an accomplished ballerina. She still, thank heavens, has her health. Yet she has only a short time to live if her HIV condition is not treated.

44

She pleaded her case in a composed manner with her interviewer: "I've got nothing to lose, so why won't the doctors let me take Virodene? I think it will do something for me. I've been on AZT and it did nothing. I felt far worse after the course of medication. I'm not interested in the three-drug-cocktail that everyone is suggesting. When you're in my condition every day is precious. Please, it's my body. Surely I should be allowed to decide if the risk is worthwhile."

Somehow, coming from her – the archetypal girl next door that every young boy dreams about – it put the whole deadly AIDS tragedy into a tangible, human perspective that no amount of statistics can succeed in doing. One wanted to cry with her mother who must have said: "It couldn't possibly have happened to my daughter." One wanted to pound the brute who transmitted the virus to her consciously or unconsciously. One wanted to ask God why if he has any influence over the course of human affairs did he allow such a cruel twist of fate to mar such a young life – allow such a personal tragedy. Above all, one felt a blind fury towards all those who argue that AIDS is Nature's way of striking back against overpopulation; or else relish the idea that it is divine retribution to punish promiscuity. Let one of their sons and daughters be infected and see if that shakes them out of such a complacent state of mind.

And don't say it won't happen to people like us. It just needs a nasty collision in rugby, a car accident, having a tooth drilled or an operation with unhygienic equipment or being stabbed in a mugging. Any incident where blood meets blood carries some probability of transmission, however remote. And the greater proportion of people who are HIV positive in South Africa, the more that probability will rise.

As I write this article, I'm looking at a picture of Princess Di shaking hands with Nelson Mandela in Cape Town. She also looks radiant in a polka-dot dress in the sunshine, and she has also had her trials and tribulations. But what continually brings out my admiration for her is that she doesn't lead an empty social existence. She's been recently campaigning for the banning of land mines which cause death and horrendous injuries to countless civilians. However, the subject of her conversation with Mandela was AIDS. How many prominent South Africans have actually sat down with the President and talked about that subject? Any?

Alas, the sad truth is that it requires the highest profile woman on Earth to visit South Africa to do what no local luminary has done to my knowledge – raise the issue of AIDS at the highest level. She physically embraces AIDS victims to allay myths and prejudices. All we do is argue over *Sarafina 2* and Virodene. Perhaps we should take the cue from Di and do something concrete ourselves to alleviate the suffering and stop the spread of AIDS.

Rwandan convent

A Rwandan convent showed that young people prosper when given security, education, health and a sound economic system. Conversely, Thomas Hobbes, the seventeenth-century philosopher asserted that when people lack a properly functioning government to keep them all in awe, "life is solitary, poor, nasty, brutish and short".

3.8.1997   At a recent dinner party in Cape Town, my eye was drawn to the most exquisite tablecloth and napkins I've ever seen. Sensing my admiration, the Belgian host explained their history. About 50 kilometres north of Kigali in Rwanda, there used to be a Roman Catholic convent. The nuns there taught local schoolgirls how to do embroidery. Their speciality was flowers and African birds.

Because of their natural aptitude for doing extremely fine and detailed work, what started out as a training programme turned into a flourishing business. Flemish linen was imported from Belgium and the girls embroidered the material using vividly coloured thread. Parrots, eagles, kingfishers, louries – they all looked as if they were about to fly out of the cloth. The final product was exported to Belgium where it fetched a considerable, though not outlandish, price. On account of the troubles in Rwanda, the convent was closed down, the talented little workforce scattered to the winds and the business was no more. But for a time it produced items of world-class quality snapped up by eager customers in Europe.

This story prompted me to do a bit of lateral thinking. What had the convent offered the girls to make them do world-class needlework? Four things: security, education, health and a sound economic system. Security did not just mean protection from physical harm. In a more general sense, the nuns provided an orderly, disciplined environment in which the girls grew in self-confidence and skill. Nothing kills skill and craftsmanship like fear and chaos. Nothing boosts it like consistent governance and a stable set of values. The girls knew exactly where they stood in the hierarchy. Like an old-fashioned monastery in medieval times, the convent was a centre of excellence – a tranquil bay in an ocean of war and instability.

The education the girls received wasn't just teaching them how to embroider – the method. It also included a whole set of spiritual values and general knowledge which allowed them to understand why they were being taught this skill – the reason. Artistry needs the combination of the "how" with the "why". For the "why" gives the meaning to work and meaningfulness inspires people to produce results which are beyond the ordinary.

Health, which normally covers shelter, clothes, food and medical care, was not all that the convent provided for the girls. The sense of community, of being part of an organisation with a higher purpose added to their wellbeing. Social interaction is as important to the progress of the individual as a healthy physical environment.

Lastly, money does make the world go round. How much the Rwandan convent received for their efforts we will never know. But it was obviously enough to create a viable community. Perhaps the convent could have existed solely on funding from the Roman Catholic church, but these additional earnings must have come in handy. Moreover, you can bet these material gains were a source of pride to both the nuns and the girls. The fact that sophisticated consumers in Western countries were prepared to shell out substantial sums for work done in a remote rural area of Rwanda gives a special twist to the tale. It runs totally counter to the endless reports of butchery, misery, refugees and corruption that emanate from this region of the African continent.

Well, you may say, the convent no longer exists so the forces of evil triumphed. The impressions given by the international television networks are therefore not misleading. Nevertheless, my thesis is that a point of light was temporarily created in the surrounding darkness by these nuns. On a microscopic scale, they demonstrated the real potential of this continent. Africa has lacked the type of honest and good government provided by the nuns. Its people have not been served well. As fish need water to survive in, citizens need such an enabling environment to become world champions in industry and commerce. Likewise, talented people only stay if the environment remains conducive and amenable. Otherwise, they set off for greener pastures. Africa can catch up with the West and the Far East. But it requires world-class government to do so.

Measurable goals

Some sort of measurable goals should be put in place in South Africa to judge whether the ruling party can be pronounced to be world class. The latest World Development Report of the World Bank supports the view that an effective state is essential for a prosperous economy. However, a survey of 3 600 entrepreneurs in 69 countries revealed that 80 per cent of the respondents in Latin America, Eastern Europe and Sub-Saharan Africa lacked confidence in the ability of the authorities to protect their property from criminals and 70 per cent said that judicial arbitrariness was a big problem for their businesses.

10.8.1997 World-class government. Although the concept is valid, few electorates in the world would vote that they actually have one. Whether it's high unemployment, rising crime, the reduction in welfare entitlements, deteriorating quality in state education and health, or the widening gap between the rich and the poor – each shortcoming is cumulative and ensures continued dissatisfaction with politicians and political parties across the planet. So many times are electoral promises broken that the odds are good for a winning party to descend into ignominy before its term of office is over. The pendulum invariably swings!

Thus, while world-class companies can be readily identified, world-class governments are a different matter altogether. Marx thought he was on to a world-class ideology with communism but it failed miserably in Stalin and Mao's hands. Socialism, as a weaker alternative, had its moment in places like Sweden but has since been ditched. As governments have become more aware of how little they control of a nation's destiny, they have become less ambitious. No more great leaps forward.

So, Thatcherism is roughly where the world is today despite the Tory loss in the UK. Blair is pretty indistinguishable from Major, and Clinton has moved to the right ever since his election as US President.

Uganda, Tanzania, Chile, Argentina, Malaysia and Thailand have joined the bandwagon too. As one learned South Africa professor of law remarked to me at a wedding the other day: "The Left has run out of ideas."

World class in the sphere of politics today, therefore, means limited government. Big government no longer qualifies. Just as world-class companies are judged by certain financial parameters, so are governments. Instead of total return to shareholders and growth in earnings per share, governments are measured directly by how much they spend. Two crucial statistics have become universally accepted as necessary to be placed in the world-class category: the budget deficit should be less than 3 per cent of GDP and government debt should be no more than 60 per cent of GDP. All European governments have to meet these targets in order to qualify for monetary union due to be introduced in 1999. More general yardsticks are an inflation rate of less than 3 per cent, an unemployment rate of less than 5 per cent, real economic growth of at least 3 per cent per annum for an advanced economy and at least 6 per cent per annum for a developing one.

More quality-of-life oriented criteria are also used to judge a government, such as a rise in life expectancy, a fall in infant mortality, an increase in literacy and numeracy among the population and a decrease in the Gini coefficient (used to measure income inequality). Lower rates of violent crime like murder and rape are looked for as well as growing rates of business start-ups and home ownership. Sophisticated accounting techniques have been introduced to see whether or not a nation's high economic growth rate has been achieved at the expense of the environment. In other words, depletion of environmental resources like the cutting down of tropical forests is now figured in as a cost in the national accounts.

An interesting development is the comparison of societies on a corruption-free scale. The Scandinavian countries and New Zealand top the pole. For many world-class companies, the absence of corruption in government is a make-or-break component of a decision to invest in a foreign country. This index is bound to be watched more closely given the number of bribery scandals hitting the headlines in virtually every corner of the earth.

Note, though, that all these more general yardsticks are not for measuring government's performance directly, but for assessing the nation's health as a whole as guided by the government. In this context, government is seen predominantly as either an empowering or a disempowering agency. A soccer manager and coach are judged in the same way. It's not what they themselves do during the training sessions or whilst sitting on the bench during the matches. To the club's fans, that's irrelevant. The only thing that counts is the performance of the players on the field and the goals for and against. A team's standing in the league is the basis on which the manager and coach are idolised or sacked.

To be perceived as a world-class government, therefore, the nation you're running has to win in the world economic stakes. You can't just pat yourself on the back for balancing the budget.

Promising environment
It's all about government creating a promising environment to help people help themselves.

29.10.1995 Let me start with one story and one quote before getting to the main purpose of this article. The story comes from Al Gore. He was in a restaurant in Washington the other day. As is customary at the beginning of a meal, the waiter brought him a bread roll and one pat of butter. Gore called the waiter over and asked if he could have one more pat of butter. The waiter refused. Gore asked: "Do you know who I am?" The waiter responded: "Yes. You are the Vice President of the United States of America but I'm in charge of the butter."

Now for the quote. It comes from James Carville who directed Bill Clinton's election campaign in 1992: "I used to think that, if there was reincarnation, I wanted to come back as the president, or the pope. But now I want to be the bond market: you can intimidate everybody."

Gore's self-deprecating story indicates the limits of power to which any government is subject today. This in turn is due to the greater self-confidence and autonomy felt by ordinary citizens in a modern democratic society. You wouldn't have behaved like the waiter in front of a medieval monarch or to be more accurate the next in line to the throne. "Off with his head" would have been the immediate command.

Carville's humorous quote, on the other hand, shows just how much the international rules of the economic game have eroded the sovereignty of individual governments. One London economist calls it "the paradox of volatile stability". Bond markets react so swiftly and so savagely to erroneous economic policies that governments through sheer fear pursue more disciplined domestic strategies. This leads to greater stability in the longer run.

How restricted is government? Take unemployment, the principal scourge everywhere. The Keynesian solution of increasing state expenditure to solve the problem now runs into one of three brick walls. Either taxes have to be increased to balance the budget and the resulting fall in jobs in the private sector negates any public job-creation programme. Or government has to borrow the money to finance the expenditure, in which case it crowds out the private sector from the savings market. Or government must print money to pay for the expenditure in which case inflation rises which scares foreign investors away and raises bond rates. From all sides, government is hemmed in.

This is not to say that government cannot exercise some power over a nation's destiny. Of course it does. But it is in the form of influence rather than control. For instance, the long-term cure for unemployment includes the encouragement of entrepreneurial education in schools, nudging financial institutions to come up with innovative ways of providing seed money for small business development, disseminating successful community programmes in the realm of job creation to the rest of the country, providing incentives for the retraining of retrenched workers and removing obstacles to a flexible labour market. These actions establish a promising environment to tackle unemployment. You can't do more.

In summary, Gore should have used his charm, and not his position, to induce the waiter to give him more butter. Carville's wish should have been to be reincarnated as a Coca-Cola advertisement. The power of persuasion leads to more lasting achievements than intimidation. That's the real thing!

Support from Botswana

This empowering role of government is supported by three star pupils from Botswana.

2.6.1996 Last Monday, I gave the keynote address at a conference organised by the Botswana Confederation of Commerce, Industry and Manpower in Francistown. The subject was employment creation. The President, the Vice President and other members of the cabinet were there along with many prominent members of the civil service and private sector.

Before I spoke, three teenagers were chosen to read short essays they had written on the topic: "Our future employment: hopes and fears of today's teenagers". First on the podium was Maleshiane Manco who is an eighteen-year-old student teacher at Camp Primary School in Gaborone. She said: "Lack of job creation leaves the whole nation disoriented. Information that is imparted through career guidance departments in schools is more theoretical than realistic in relation to job-market requirements. We should be advised on appropriate subjects in order to be marketable.

"When we, the youth, are faced with the pressure of lack of employment we easily divert into such immoral activities as drug trafficking and abuse, organised crime, youth gangs and even prostitution. Such activities are headed by manipulative and malicious organised criminals who abuse youth, or take advantage of them for economic and political gains. These activities will leave our government at a loss since a lot of money will be allocated to stop their occurrence. Good policies do exist in Botswana but what seems to be lacking are well-directed, action-oriented programmes."

Second up was Boingotlo Marope, a seventeen-year-old pupil at Gaborone Secondary School. She said: "People with Master's degrees cannot find employment. In the past a person with such qualifications could be a Minister. Nowadays they are roaming the streets in search of employment. In ten years' time, people with these qualities will most probably be cleaning the streets. The spiralling crime wave that has been gripping the nation is costing us a lot. Such kind of behaviour is not acceptable to the investors. It chases them away. These investors help in job creation. If crime is not reduced there will be a reduction in employment. Drought-relief projects should be broadened so that the unskilled/uneducated can also make a living."

Third was Zenzele Hirschfeld, a fifteen-year-old student at Marang Community Junior Secondary School. She said: "Looking at the negative side of things, one is most likely going to conclude that the job market is unable to absorb all school-leavers because the economy of the country is growing at a slow pace. This problem is going to be with us for quite some time. What needs to be done is to train today's youth in such a way that they can make a living in the informal sector. Instead of equipping our teenagers with only academic skills, let us give them technical skills as well.

"Teenagers with technical skills are most likely to create jobs not only for themselves, but for other members of society. The government and the private sectors can never create enough jobs for all of us. The government should try to create the right atmosphere for those with foresight to develop self-employing projects. The problem with today's youth is that they believe at the end of their schooling the government owes them jobs. This is not the case. All that the government should do is to prepare us to be competitive in the job market. The whole world has a shortage of technically qualified people. Our government and the private sector must help by sponsoring more students in this field. It is also up to teenagers to develop more interest in subjects such as mathematics, science, technical drawing, etc. Without the youth, the lifespan of both the government and the private sector is limited. So we need your attention in the same way as you need ours. Not today, but yesterday."

Everything these three very bright young people said is relevant for us here. Are you listening?

Disappearing taxpayers
Because of the risk of the disappearing taxpayer, a government has to be lean and cost-effective.

17.8.1997 Jean-Baptiste Colbert was treasurer to Louis XIV, King of France. His advice to the sovereign on financial matters was as follows:

54

"The art of taxation consists in so plucking the goose to obtain the largest amount of feathers, with the least possible amount of hissing." *The Economist* drew readers' attention to this quote in its excellent leader recently on "the disappearing taxpayer".

As the journal commented: "Colbert's observation remains true, except for one big change. Unlike geese, people in the 17th century did not know how to fly. Now they can. In the coming decades electronic commerce – combined with the growing ease with which firms can shift their operations from one part of the world to another – will make it even easier for people to flee countries where taxes are high, or to evade taxes altogether by doing their business in cyberspace."

In our 1986 scenario study, we listed "low taxation" as one of the principal characteristics of a "winning nation". Apart from anything else, it improved the work ethic of a country because people kept what they earned. However, with the increasing mobility of capital, companies and skilled people as the world approaches the new millennium, this aspect has assumed an overriding importance. Even goods can be purchased via the Internet from countries with the lowest VAT rates. So, a race to the bottom may be in the offing as countries vie with one another to lower taxes in order to attract trade, foreign direct investment and qualified immigrants.

In a sense, the new triumvirate of technology, liberalisation and globalisation will have as much impact on world-class governments as it is having on world-class companies. The latter are already facing falling real prices for virtually all their products in the wake of hypercompetition with no respect for borders.

If tax is considered to be the price that citizens pay for law and order, monetary stability and infrastructure, we may be in for a "taxpayers' market" on account of intergovernmental competition. Right now, a widespread disparity in taxes still exists. For example, the top marginal rate on personal income tax in Sweden is almost 60 per cent, which an individual reaches at an annual income of $28 000, while in America the ceiling is 40 per cent at a threshold of $260 000. German corporate tax is close to 60 per cent compared to Switzerland at 30 per cent. VAT in Sweden runs at 25 per cent against 5 per cent in the US and Japan. A downward convergence is likely as pressure mounts on governments to satisfy footloose and fancy-free entrepreneurs and consumers who are prone to go to tax havens if obliged to do so.

In South Africa, we already have the problem of persuading people who in the past did not pay their rates and taxes to stump up the money now. The campaign so far has not been successful. However, in light of the foregoing trends, the risk for the South African government of relying on a narrow base of wealthy individuals and companies for their tax revenue must be obvious. They are the skein of geese that can fly away.

Similarities between world-class companies and government

Who would have thought that a world-class government and a world-class company have lots in common? But a world-class government should focus on only those things that the private sector cannot do. Whilst in the article I state that education and health are two functions in which the state should be involved, one can debate the nature of that involvement. The actual construction and running of state schools and hospitals could easily be delegated to the private sector, with the funding of these activities being the responsibility of government. If such complete devolution is unacceptable, a halfway house would be to make the PTAs and hospital boards as autonomous as university authorities. On a different front, given that many of the best advocates and attorneys are in private legal firms, perhaps the state should outsource the prosecution of some cases to them.

24.8.1997 Governments and big companies have a lot more in common than either would care to admit. They both deliver products and services to the public and should do so in a quality-driven, cost-effective way. They both manage a large body of employees – a civil service on the one hand and a workforce on the other – and should do so in a just and inspirational manner. They both have competitors. In the case of a government, it's not only opposition parties they have to worry about, it's other governments as well which are all trying to attract the lion's share of foreign direct investment to their countries.

New Zealand has acknowledged the similarity. Each government department is now treated like an autonomous business, the chief executive of which is equivalent to the director-general here. The CE is on a fixed-term contract so that he can be turfed out in the event of nonperformance. The Minister in charge of the portfolio is somewhat akin to an executive chairman of a company. He still carries overall responsibility for the function but has delegated the day-to-day running of the organisation to the CE. Indisputably, New Zealand is a better-run country as a result of these changes. That's why it's referred to as New Zealand Inc.

If a government wishes to be world class, then it has to comply with virtually all the principles that apply to a world-class company and more. Let me repeat the attributes by which the most admired companies are ranked in the US in the annual survey undertaken by *Fortune*: innovation; quality of management; community and environmental responsibility; ability to attract, develop and keep talented people; quality of products and services; financial soundness and use of corporate assets. The only one that sounds out of place for a government is value as a long-term investment, because a government does not have shareholders and does not make a profit as such.

I would like to single out the issue of talented people. If government wants them in the civil service and other organs of government, it has to indulge in a tug-of-war with the private sector. While the latter can offer share options and the chance of making a fortune, the civil service et al. can only pay a basic salary plus fringe benefits. There has to be something extra – an esprit de corps, a feeling that you've joined an elite band of men and women with the noble ideal of serving their country. In order to assemble this competent core of human beings for civic duties, pride and money are both crucial. France has special schools and universities at which students with potential to rise to the upper echelons of the civil service are trained.

But the remuneration aspect demands that the total number of government employees remains small. You cannot pay well, keep taxation within international norms and have millions on the payroll all at the same time. So the next step is for government to focus on doing only those activities which the private sector can't do and shed all the others. It must be accepted that a basic choice is being made here: either a government pursues the objective of being world class by getting the requisite talent or it remains an employer of last resort. It cannot satisfy both objectives.

So privatisation is essential if a government wants to end up with a small world-class civil service which is highly motivated and properly remunerated. Because of modern technology, virtually no monopolies exist today which the state has to own in order to protect the public. That reason has vanished. Post Offices are up against fax machines, wired telephones against cellulars, railways against taxis and trucks, airlines against other airlines, state radio and TV against private radio and TV stations. The whole lot should be in private hands. Competition will ensure that the consumer gets a fair deal, and probably a better one than he is currently getting from the state. The only exception I can think of is electricity where no alternative exists for a modern household. Even that can be sold off by the government if prices are subsequently regulated by an ombudsman appointed to represent consumer interests.

What does that leave for government to do besides its core activity of legislation? Primarily law and order, defence, education, health and finance (which includes targeted welfare for the really needy above what is already being done by the NGOs). The two key questions that a government should ask itself are the same as those which test the minds of the leaders of world-class businesses: what can I focus on which is not being done by anybody else out there in the market and how can I do it best?

Smart partnerships

An effective government seeks smart partnerships with the private sector where both sides win. Museveni's speech at SAID '97 indicated that the "winds of change" are once again blowing through Africa. A new generation of leaders is replacing the immediate postcolonial ones. Such men are more interested in looking forward to better times than blaming the past for the current state of affairs. Focus is a driving force behind a smart regional partnership, with each country specialising in what it's best at and exporting to the others. The principle makes a lot of sense in Southern Africa, where each country has its own comparative advantages, e.g. in climate and rainfall, natural resources or manufacturing capacity.

11.5.1997 It's a pity that South African government ministers as well as the media have missed out on the most significant event in Africa's recent economic history. The event was the First Southern Africa International Dialogue on "Smart Partnership for the Generation of Wealth". SAID '97 took place at Kasane in Botswana from 4 to 7 May. It was a unique dialogue between heads of state and the private sector. Ten leaders attended from Botswana, Zimbabwe, Namibia, Malawi, Mozambique, Ghana, Tanzania, Uganda, South Africa and Malaysia – as well as 220 other delegates including myself.

Although Nelson Mandela was there only fleetingly because of the Zaïre talks, it was an unbelievable experience. During the interactive sessions, the Presidents sat with all of us at the tables debating the philosophy and practice of smart partnership, the development of Southern Africa as a growth area and the roles of government, the private sector and labour in making it all happen. I doubt whether anywhere in the world there has ever been an informal forum with such public access to so many top decision-makers in one fell swoop. I even got them all to autograph a menu!

Smart partnership is a concept born out of a perceived need in Malaysia that the public sector should aid and abet the private sector in the fulfilment of economic goals. It involves the creation of "win-win" working relationships, where all partners benefit over the long term and develop a cooperative spirit. The critical point is that each partner needs to perceive it as being to its own advantage for the smart partnership to persist. For this reason many current partnerships are not smart. Smart partnerships evolve naturally through osmosis, based as they are on common sense. Within countries, between countries within a geographical region and worldwide between regions, they are growing in number – particularly in light of the globalisation of business.

The outstanding contributions to the dialogue forums came from Dr Mahathir, the Prime Minister of Malaysia, and Messrs Museveni and Mkapa, Presidents of Uganda and Tanzania respectively. Mahathir forged a deep bond with the gathering with his clarion call for South-South partnerships in order to counterbalance the economically dominant North. Museveni and Mkapa gave no-nonsense portrayals of what it takes to be a winning nation in a highly competitive world. The government should be the facilitator by focusing on providing infrastructure like roads, schools and hospitals and a business-friendly framework. The latter includes one-stop investment service centres and multiple-entry visas for foreign investors, currency convertibility, low inflation, low taxation, security of property, law and order, a civil service retrained to be supportive of business, and a corruption-free environment. The private sector is the engine of growth. A productive labour force, knowledgeable of the national priorities, is the third ingredient.

Museveni specifically talked of the "sovereignty" of business. While the world consisted of generous and selfish people, the majority were in the second category and therefore propelled by self-interest. Given that hard fact, they performed better when left to do their own thing (including the formation of smart partnerships). It was quite apparent that the Presidents of the economies which had suffered the most pain had the clearest vision and conviction of the way forward. Sort of "been there, done that. Now let's get down to brass tacks."

Readers may groan about just another gigantic, unnecessary and expensive talk-fest with taxpayers' money being consumed on the fuel of the presidential jets. They would be mistaken. I got the distinct impression that this was a historic turning point in Africa's chequered economic history. The New Africa is emerging. And to make sure the renaissance is for real, all participants including the leaders committed themselves to an action programme based on the principle of smart partnerships. A report-back and further dialogue will take place at SAID '98 in Namibia. Cyril Ramaphosa, a co-chairman of SAID '97, concluded the event with the exhortation: "Now to move from contact to contract."

Violent kids

Violent kids represent the greatest challenge to a democratic society with aspirations to world-class tranquillity.

15.12.1996   When you next stare down the barrel of an AK47 owned by a fourteen-year-old about to relieve you of your BMW, spare a thought for him. He's a global phenomenon. Just another disoriented postmodernist kid that I profile in *The High Road: Where are we now?*

What is postmodernism? Before I define it, let's look at modernism. The latter spanned 230 years from the beginning of the industrial revolution in the 1750s to the 1980s. It was associated with people collecting in ever-larger organisations to mass-produce hard objects like cars and televisions. The zenith of modernism was the 1950s when half of the American population worked on production lines. Now services constitute 70 per cent of America's GDP and the reverse is happening: people are dispersing into smaller businesses. Society is atomising and power is shifting down to the individual.

All the certainties we had in the 1950s are therefore no longer relevant in the 1990s. For example, I knew way back then that I would have a mother who would stay at home and a father who would go out to work. I knew I'd get smacked if I did something wrong. I knew that when I left school, I would get a job working for someone somewhere. Now kids are surprised to have a mother and a father; Dr Spock rules about never smacking a child; and there's absolutely no guarantee – in fact very little likelihood – that you'll get a job, even with good grades in your examinations. Anyway, a lot of kids drop out early to while away their lives on the streets.

Parentless, jobless, bored, undisciplined kids spell big trouble. In the US, the fastest growing homicide rate is among juveniles, fourteen to seventeen years old. In Britain, citizens no longer complain of socialism but the antisocialism of youth. Teachers have to go on strike

61

to get disruptive pupils removed from school. In South Africa, three seventeen-year-olds recently blew away one of South Africa's top black equestrians as he was leaving a show-jumping event at Kyalami – for the car he was driving. What a waste of a human life!

It's not that the majority of kids have become violent and evil. It's probably the same minority as it ever was. But that minority are no longer kept in control by society. They are in charge. They assert themselves by bullying the rest and taking other people's lives if necessary. "I kill therefore I am" is the ultimate form of self-expression. No retribution – human or divine – now exists to restrain them. No moral commandment guides them. Everything is excusable. Welcome to *Lord of the Flies*.

New Age idealists believe that the postmodernist world is a cool, hip place to be. Yes, it is more individualistic and creative. But without any stable ethical frame of reference, it is also very scary, brutal and chaotic. Several African states have become "kidocracies". Who can forget those pictures of barefoot Liberian tots in raggedy T-shirts spraying pedestrians with state-of-the-art automatic weaponry? No cyberspace for them where a mouse click starts the game over again. They trade in actual reality where real bodies get pumped full of real holes leaving real bloodstains on the dusty streets.

As I said at the beginning, this terrifying trend of dead-eyed children who show no remorse and no self-restraint is universal. It is not, as many people feel, confined to South Africa. As adults, we are not alone in feeling vulnerable in the face of postmodernism.

Drugs and sex
We can never become world class if our kids indulge in drugs and sex.

2.3.1997   Three related items give rise to this week's column. The first was a section of *Carte Blanche* broadcast on M-Net last weekend. A group of South African high school pupils were asked to watch an American movie called *Kids* and give their reactions. The film, having been banned last year, had the ban recently lifted on the grounds that the content had educational value.

The plot centres on the lives of some ordinary American teenagers in an urban setting. No stars were used; the actors and actresses were hired off the streets. Basically, the movie reveals in a no-holds-barred manner just how much teenagers swear, take drugs and have promiscuous sex as they go about their daily existence. Derek Watts then asked the audience whether the movie was true to life in South Africa. Several of the children confirmed that the language and actions they had seen perfectly mirrored their experiences here. How young, Derek asked them, are South African kids when they first have sex? He got answers all the way down to twelve. He then put the issue of AIDS and the risk of unprotected sex on the table. One girl scoffed at the idea of using a condom. Basically, the theme from a fair number of the responses (there were exceptions) was that it is smart to indulge in licentious behaviour at the earliest possible age and adults should be taught that this is perfectly cool and okay.

The second item was the lead story on Radio 702 news on Wednesday morning. It concerned drugs being freely available to kids in their early teens in Lenasia. The pushers have become role models to Lenasia's youth because of their expensive clothes and cars. The third item was an announcement the same morning by a deejay on squeaky-clean Highveld Stereo that one of his three all-time favourite songs was "Cocaine". An interesting comment, coming hot on the heels of the news about proliferating drugs in Lenasia.

So we must ask ourselves: are young South Africans really going to descend into a round of psychedelic, hedonistic orgies interspersed with swear words that would bring a blush even to the cheeks of hardened regulars at the bars on the docks? Of course, one should widen the question and ask whether we are merely part of the global phenomenon of postmodernism with its moral relativism and nihilistic values. Drugs, for example, are now the second largest business in the world – after tourism and before defence. The top 25 Mafia families in America made $64 billion out of drugs last year, before and after tax. Putting that into perspective, each family earned on average $2,5 billion, which is equivalent to R11 billion. If you add the other rackets like prostitution and gambling, one Mafia family pulls in more than three times Anglo's bottom-line profit.

I don't want to sound like Mother Grundy but somehow we have to attack the proposition that it is cool to swear, have sex and take drugs at the age of twelve. Perhaps, as *The Economist* proposes, we should legalise drugs to get them out of the hands of criminals and then mount a public campaign about the dangers of using them. After all, sex workers and pornography are legal now. Tobacco and alcohol have been legal for years. At least we would then have all-round consistency in terms of vices that can harm us.

Nevertheless, the message should be given to the younger generation over and over again: when you're washed up at the age of nineteen with a fried brain, a used body, terminal AIDS and the ability only to mutter "f– off" incoherently, that ain't cool. That's heavy.

Family values

The promotion of family values is therefore an important aspect of government policy. "Quality time" is used as an excuse not to spend enough time with your children. Like a business, rearing a family needs focus. Unfortunately, many yuppie couples regard home as work and work as home.

18.7.1995 *Families in Focus* is a study recently released by the Population Council, an international family-planning group based in New York. It states that divorce rates have increased substantially in virtually every developed country since 1970. In France, West Germany, Netherlands, Hungary and the Czech Republic 30 per cent of marriages break up. In Canada, Britain, Denmark and Sweden the figure hovers around 40 per cent. In the US the figure is over 50 per cent, though it has dropped from 60 per cent in 1980. Only Italy and Greece still have a low marriage break-up rate – around 10 per cent but rising.

In addition, the percentage of children born to unmarried mothers has grown in all countries (except Japan) where statistics are available. In North Europe and the US, the figure is around 30 per cent. An obvious conclusion of the study is that children in one-parent homes – normally with a mother as head of the household – are far more likely to be living in poverty than children in two-parent homes. Even in two-parent homes, children are less well looked after than they were twenty years ago because more frequently both parents have jobs outside the home. Sweden, despite its advanced state policies for family support, has not managed to keep the family intact. In fact, some would argue that entitlements for single parents can actually induce marital break-up.

The *Newsweek* article from which I gleaned all this information is aptly headed "Life without Father". I will never forget in one of my earliest "High Road" lectures in Cape Town in 1987 having an interchange with a member of the audience on this issue. I had just reached the part about the characteristics of a "winning nation" and how one of them was a work ethic. In turn, one of the conditions for a work ethic was a sound family system, because this produced children who at the age of eighteen were ready and willing to contribute to society. This elicited the comment that I was completely ignoring all those courageous single mothers in South Africa who were bringing up their children just fine. My response was that whilst I had whole-hearted respect for these mothers, one could not seriously doubt that being brought up by a mother and a father was better than being brought up by a mother alone.

At the time I lacked any evidence to support this thesis. But a report published a couple of years ago in Britain showed that children from two-parent homes were consistently higher achievers at school than children from single-parent homes. Moreover, children from broken homes (where the parents had divorced) did not do as well as children from families where one or other parent had died. The emotional trauma of a divorce psychologically scars children more than the loss of a parent.

So how do we reverse the destruction of the nuclear family? It's not easy when you have the full weight of Hollywood culture against you. Heroes in movies tend to be single, divorced or separated but never boringly married. The cult of the stud making his score with one woman after another but seldom forging a lasting relationship continues. It's as though Hollywood remains locked in the time warp of the free-loving 1960s. On the other hand, one can argue that Hollywood is merely serving up what the younger generation still want to see. If the values of the latter changed, Hollywood would too. It's hard to know which is the chicken and which is the egg.

Nevertheless, youngsters are altering their attitudes. The threat of

AIDS, the rejection of 1980s materialism for a more meaningful lifestyle in the 1990s, the growing popularity of fundamentalist religious movements are slowly but surely changing the sexual mores of the young. As mentioned earlier, the divorce rate in America is dropping. Moreover, laws are being passed in several countries to compel fathers who leave home to support their kids or face dire penalties. Not that legislation makes a happy home, but it does send the message to irresponsible males that they can't just have their pleasure and run.

Despite the pessimism of the survey by the Population Council, I detect a swing in the pendulum back towards celibacy and monogamy which is not yet reflected in the statistics. Just as the children of the 50's generation rebelled against the staidness of their parents and the nuclear family, so the children of the post-60's generation do not want to repeat the "hippie" habits and casual relationships of their parents. It would be too much to say, though, that we will return to Frank Sinatra's "love and marriage, go together like a horse and carriage".

Personal accountability
But we all need to learn about personal accountability to be world-class individuals.

19.5.1996 I came across an interesting comparison the other day concerning the top seven disciplinary problems in American schools. The source was the Congressional Quarterly of November 1993. It is now a slide in my latest scenario presentation, *"The High Road – Ten Years On"*.

In 1940 the list comprised: talking out of turn, chewing gum, making a noise, running in hallways, queue-jumping, ignoring the dress code and littering. In 1990 a similar list was as follows: drug abuse, alcohol abuse, sexual behaviour, (attempted) suicide, rape and sexual assault, robbery and theft, and physical assault.

The contrast is stunning, isn't it? The Pearl Harbour attack only occurred on 7 December 1941, so one can't even use the excuse that in 1940 America was at war, and therefore more disciplined, for the difference. The fact is that, using a baseline of half a century, values have shown a marked decline among the youth in the US. Impolite transgressions on school grounds have been replaced by criminal acts. Not unsurprisingly, the issue of values is set to dominate this year's presidential campaign. Books like *Values Matter Most* by Ben Wattenberg and *Book of Virtues* by William Bennett have ridden high in the American charts.

What on earth has caused this sad state of affairs? I would hazard the following answer. Children are no longer taught absolute moral truths. We live in a world where everything is qualified and relative. "Thou shalt not" has been transformed into "under certain circumstances thou shalt be excused". An expert can easily be found to provide convenient external reasons for misconduct. Individual accountability thereby goes out of the window. Moreover, religious teaching at home and in school has waned in importance. Hellfire and damnation no longer figure in the minds of the young. Divine justice in the form of an Old Testament God does not stop immoral acts. To make matters worse, retribution of the human kind is now frowned upon. If little Johnny is behaving like a brute, the new philosophy is that he should be encouraged to change, not disciplined.

Into the vacuum left by the absence of sanctions against unacceptable behaviour, the idea of instant gratification has stepped. It used to be that cake was only offered after you had finished the brown bread. Now it is the case of "I want it all and I want it now". This starts with toys but moves on to sex and drugs. Self-denial and abstinence are considered foolish. You're a nerd if you don't go with the flow.

Today's *Zeitgeist* is that children – and parents for that matter – are victims of social forces beyond their control. The cause of teenage delinquency is variously put down to the breakdown of the family, changing work patterns which keep parents away from home, too much television, violent or suggestive pop lyrics, the stress of cramped urban lives or the prevalence of drugs and alcohol. But kids and parents both have a choice. Kids don't have to watch too much television: parents don't have to let them. Kids don't have to accept drugs and alcohol: parents can vet the parties their kids go to. Kids don't have to react violently in difficult situations: parents can teach them moral values.

Luckily, during the time since the list of disciplinary problems was published in 1990, there has been an inkling of a turnaround. American teenagers are taking more responsibility for their own actions, family values are receiving greater attention, robbery and assault incur harsher penalties from the state and religious movements are becoming increasingly popular among the young. Some of the hottest-selling CDs are to be found in the gospel music section. So the cycle may be turning and ethics may be reviving. But it is too early to say whether the forces of decadence have been truly vanquished.

Rethinking defence
To be world class, government needs to rethink the role of defence.

5.11.1995 *Newsweek* gave its interview with him earlier this year the headline "Wars of the 21st Century". BBC's Panorama called his vision *Pulp Future*. A car bomb in Oklahoma City, a seemingly deliberate train derailment near Phoenix, Arizona, bombs in Paris metros make him something of a prophet. Suddenly Martin Van Crefeld, a 49-year-old mild-mannered military historian at the Hebrew University of Jerusalem, is one of the most sought-after specialists on the future of warfare. The audiences he has lectured to include senior British officers, American special forces and the CIA. The reason he's such a hot property is that his opinions make the current defence strategies of many nations obsolete.

His basic thesis is that future wars are unlikely to be fought between states in the same way they have been fought in the past. World War II was fought with large armies in set-piece battles, with tanks and big artillery pieces backing up the infantry, with squadrons of planes bombing the enemy's territory and with fleets of ships and submarines seeking domination of the oceans. Now, he says, the threat to a modern state is not the possibility of World War III. It comes from the increasing powerlessness of a state against various anarchic trends inside and outside its borders.

The most important internal trend is the destabilising effect of sub-national organisations carving out empires of their own within each state. Such organisations include clans, terrorist groups, religious cults, private militias, urban gangs and rural bandits. Cheap but effective weaponry is available to all of them. A state today has more chance of slipping into internal anarchy, as a result of its power being sucked away by these organisations, than of being invaded and crushed by alien armies.

Van Crefeld backs up this view with the observation that of the approximately thirty wars being fought around the world today, none are between states. Rival subnational organisations have caused conflicts in Bosnia, Somalia, Angola, Kurdistan, Sri Lanka and Rio de Janeiro. Why the last? "Because the other day the Brazilian government sent its army into the barrios in order to reoccupy them. Most of that city is out of bounds for the government." Panorama's *Pulp Future* provides harrowing sequences of the degeneration of life not only in Rio but also in Shanghai, Liverpool and Sierra Leone. As one middle-aged Liverpool lady said in a discussion on the rising savagery in that city: "There is no law, there's no order."

The principal external threat to a state nowadays is massive infiltration by illegal immigrants fleeing the chaos of their own countries. Van Crefeld reckons that of the 200 or so sovereign states in the world today, only two dozen can be regarded as well governed and stable. While stable states have always been in a minority, in the days of the Cold War they dominated unstable regions – particularly those in their vicinity. Now they don't. This disappearance of authority, together with porous borders, opens the floodgates. Albanians pour into Italy, South and Central Americans into the United States. One Italian coastguard being interviewed in *Pulp Future* said that refugees would even risk making the voyage in seas which were too rough for the coastguard's far more seaworthy vessels to handle.

To buttress his point about the irrelevance of most modern, heavy weapons, Van Crefeld cites the example of a nuclear device falling into the hands of a terrorist group; or, as actually happened in a Tokyo subway, poison gas being released in a place where many people congregate. What is needed is brilliant detective work and undercover agents to ferret the criminals out and elite antiterror units to arrest them.

However, as Van Crefeld wryly remarks, the heads of the regular armed forces are not yet ready anywhere to admit to these changing circumstances. After all, it could place their jobs and their defence budgets in jeopardy. So what should military strategists be doing now to prepare? Van Crefeld's answer to *Newsweek* was: "They should resign themselves to becoming policemen. But most of them don't."

Bobbies on the beat

And we need more bobbies on the beat as I requested in a Christmas message to the State President. It looks as if my wish may be granted in Johannesburg. Moreover, I'm grateful for the unexpected gift of the appointment of Meyer Kahn as Chief Executive of the SAPS. He is as tough and intelligent as they come in business. I have found that out from serving on the South African Breweries board under his chairmanship for some time. If anybody can, he'll put some extra fizz into the fuzz! Remember the Western The Magnificent Seven. *The seven heroes put backbone back into an oppressed Mexican community who then fought back against the outlaws. We need the same change in spirit. Crime stands between us and the goal of being world class. It can be done. The murders in New York, Houston and Los Angeles dropped by 56 per cent, 54 per cent and 30 per cent between 1990 and 1996. America shows you can be democratic and firm at the same time.*

22.12.1996 If Nelson Mandela were Santa Claus and we were allowed to send letters up the chimney to him, mine would read as follows:

DEAR MR MANDELA,

I am now too old for toys in my stocking, but I would like to make a request for a Christmas present on behalf of all South Africans. Please, in 1997, would you and the current government take one particular step to improve law and order which I personally favour. I know that you and your ministers, the judiciary and police of all ranks are committed to reduce crime in our beloved country, so this letter is in no way trying to point fingers about the past. It is wholly concerned with the future.

The government's New Year's resolution should be to turn as many police as possible into bobbies on the beat. Like those in London, there should be pairs of them walking in the streets of all our business and residential areas at regular intervals. Particularly, they should maintain a continuous physical presence at those busy intersections where car hijackings and robberies frequently take place. Unless absolutely necessary, they should not carry firearms because this does not convey the image of a friendly bobby. They should rather carry walkie-talkies linked to roving squad cars which do have the police with the guns. There must be sufficient cars for response times to any call for help by a bobby to be a maximum of a few minutes.

South African bobbies should operate on the "broken window" principle so popular and successful in New York. No offence is too trivial not to merit attention. If bobbies curb the small crimes, it will create a positive ethos in the community to bring down the incidence of more serious crimes as well.

If there are not enough men and women on active duty in the police to cover all the streets, then as many of the administrative functions as possible within the police force should be privatised. Instead of making all those young men fill out charge sheets at the police station, why not put them on patrol and have those functions fulfilled by retired clerks who want to supplement their pension? If you still do not have sufficient manpower to deploy as bobbies, perhaps you could consider retraining army personnel to undertake these duties. After all, we do not have any external enemy at the moment to keep the SANDF fully occupied. Our chief enemy right now is internal and it is crime.

The objective is to saturate every neighbourhood of every city with men and women in blue. As for maintaining in good order the fleet of cars to prowl the streets as back-up for the bobbies, I would again respectfully suggest that this function should be put out to tender to the private sector. We are very willing to go into partnership with the state to produce a police force which is the envy of Africa. If we succeed, we will not have to build more prisons to overcome overcrowding, nor will we have to expand the number of courts to deal with the log jam of cases. Why? Because the physical presence of bobbies everywhere will deter young people from committing crimes in the first place. The exercise would therefore be very cost effective.

I know you're not the real Santa Claus but you are the State President. You can make things happen.

Merry Christmas and Happy New Year from all of us.

Yours

Clem Sunter

World-class SAPS
But some of our police are world class already.

9.4.1995 It's an experience too many people share in South Africa. Earlier this year, I returned to where I had parked my car in a shopping mall parkade – only to find it gone. I did the usual trek around the various parking levels on the basis that my memory about the exact place I had parked the car was tricking me. Bewilderment preceded fury which was followed by resignation. I got a lift to the local police station.

While filling in the forms, I played one scenario to myself. The car was permanently gone. I was going through the motions of reporting the theft as a precondition for making an insurance claim. The following day, my colleagues at the office confirmed my gloomy view. I was informed that 40 per cent of new cars of my make had already been stolen (a statistic I haven't bothered to check out). Variations on the "gone" theme were given at the drop of a hat.

My car was in a container bound for Maputo, Dar es Salaam or Lobito. It would be auctioned in the next few weeks in Nairobi. It was being used because of its speed to carry contraband to Francistown. It would be sighted in a few months' time in Auckland or Wellington, New Zealand. It was at this very moment being dismantled in a chop shop, a few kilometres as the crow flies in any direction from my office. On and on, the litany of possibilities went, each one given with mock sympathy. I learnt one thing: bad news of this nature travels fast around the office!

I put in my insurance claim. I was visited by a private detective acting on behalf of the insurance company who implied that, given the elapsed time since the theft, the odds on my getting my car back were negligible. I ordered a new car, a more downmarket model which criminals might overlook. And then I got a call from the Brixton Vehicle Theft Unit. They thought they had my car.

Indeed it was my car. A small "ding" above the passenger front wheel which I had unsuccessfully painted over clinched the identification. The system had worked. From the constable who took my details at the local police station to the warrant officer who signed the release papers on my car at Brixton, the police had done a superb job. When I saw how comprehensive the investigation had been, how professionally the case had been handled, I realised how wrong the perception is that many members of the public have of the police. They are a dedicated bunch. Your case is given personal attention.

Sad it is, then, that they are so badly paid. When the young warrant officer in the Brixton Car Theft Unit told me his monthly take-home pay for a job which combines intelligent detective work with moments of physical danger, I shuddered. That crack little unit, which with the right resources could save the insurance companies millions of rands, must be in danger of breaking up. Officers will simply drift off into the private sector and do private security work for better remuneration.

As you may gather, I am a fan of the SAPS. I do not support go-slows or strikes in their ranks. But with fifty murders a day making South Africa the number one murder nation on earth (with more than twice the per capita murder rate of the second-ranked Caribbean island of St Lucia), the police are the most important aspect of government today. Treat the men and women on the beat badly and the criminals will make life even more hazardous than it is already. We need communities to respect the constables, as they "prowl the empty streets at night". Taking the life of a policeman or policewoman should be the most serious crime that can be committed with the most severe penalties attached.

Go to London, go to Melbourne, go to most major cities which are considered safe and you will find a far stronger visible police presence than we have here. Every 500 metres, a couple of constables will be on foot patrol – talking to pedestrians, checking shops, watching out for potential crime.

Our attitude to the SAPS needs a radical shift. We need an elite police force that is highly trained, well paid and predominantly in the field. It should probably be double the size of the present complement to get close to Western ratios per head of population. Minimum force requires lots of people to enforce the law. Where is the money to come from? A massive cut in the overheads of government.

Ten Commandments

These are Edouard Parker's Ten Commandments to create a world-class economy. If you get the formula right, you can make the transition very quickly. Britain took 163 years to increase its per capita income eightfold. South Korea achieved it in a generation. We have not quite two years till "Wham" – What happens after Mandela? It will be a much easier transition if his successor inherits a going concern. A gram of hope is worth infinitely more than a ton of despair.

15.10.1995 Edouard Parker is the Executive Chairman of Société XA-EP (Études Prospectives Internationales), a consulting group based in Paris. As one of Europe's foremost political risk analysts, he specialises in elaborating scenarios on specific countries and providing companies with advice on international strategies. In over twenty years, his group has covered fifty countries. In other words, he knows what he's talking about.

In 1990, Société XA-EP carried out a global scenario study, "The State of the World and the International Business Environment at the Beginning of the 21st Century". This work introduced the "Ten Commandments" for the rapid economic development of poor countries. Let us go through the commandments one by one.

1 *Popular support and deliberate government commitment to making fast economic growth the overriding policy priority.* Parker defines "fast" as that level at which, allowing for population and productivity increases, unemployment really starts to fall. Anything less and the gap between the haves and have-nots rises inexorably.
2 *Establishment of a clear and respected legal system, especially in relation to company law and investment codes.* Investors want stable rules of the game in the countries where they intend to invest.
3 *Integration in the world economy through export growth, particularly exports of manufactured goods.* A prime driving force behind growth is a "can do" spirit among a nation's citizens that extends beyond

national boundaries. Their marketplace is the world, not just the domestic economy.

4 *Deregulation of wages, especially at the bottom of the earnings scale (however distasteful that may appear)*. To begin with, the objective of rapid growth is to benefit the least well off by job creation. Ultimately, it should raise everybody's living standards.

5 *Deregulation of prices which can then play their proper information role, signalling relative scarcity*. Resources can be most efficiently allocated by the value put on them in voluntary deals between buyers and sellers.

6 *Creation of a virtuous circle of higher savings/investment*. Without inducing people to save, a country will never have enough capital for its needs. High interest rates will discourage entrepreneurs from betting on new ventures.

7 *Small government, totally dedicated to economic success.* By small government, Parker does not mean weak government. He means a government that limits its size and its role in the economy, yet is highly supportive of the process of industrialisation.

8 *Integration of educated young people in the economic system.* Parker's concern is that if the intellectual elite of a country are not part of the wealth-creation process, they have the ability to hinder it or even stop it altogether.

9 *Increased interdependence among nations.* Parker is aiming this commandment at the rich nations, basically challenging them to open their markets to developing countries or face billions of have-nots on their doorstep.

10 *A modicum of sensible economic management.* Parker's tenth commandment emphasises that no special talent is required to become a dragon like South Korea or Singapore. Even the poorest country can pick itself up if it has the will to become a "winning nation" and a sufficient consensus about how to get there.

With these Ten Commandments, Parker is offering a stark choice to countries like South Africa. Either accept (and ultimately fulfil) the goal of fast economic growth or face the consequences of an increasing number of have-nots. If you're not a dragon, you will have chaos. There is no muddling-through scenario.

Kimberley and Johannesburg

You may recall that we once had an entrepreneurial economy before the shutters of bureaucracy came down. Business needs government as a cheerleader, not as an impediment. Think of how the Boks would play if they had a coach who didn't believe in rugby.

19.3.1995 As we debate the nature of the new constitution – unitary, federalist, confederalist, etc. – I prefer to think back to when South Africa had its greatest burst of entrepreneurial energy. This occurred between 1868 and 1900 when the diamond pipes and the gold fields were discovered and began to be exploited.

Kimberley and Johannesburg were dusty towns full of prospectors and miners and people setting up businesses to satisfy their needs. Charles Glass, Diamond Lil and lesser known brewers, striptease artistes, hoteliers, millers, retailers, weavers, cardsharps and horse race organisers co-mingled to create a riotous, spontaneous GDP growth rate which was probably in double figures for one or two decades.

The front pages of newspapers were devoted to advertisements by people selling their products and services to the market at large. The goings-on of politicians were described in later pages. They simply didn't matter as much as business. Conferences, forums and work-shops were extremely rare because the time people spent away from their livelihoods was usually taken up in carousing at pubs and dance halls, watching public spectacles, confessing their sins in church and sleeping at home.

Omniscient bureaucracies to bring order to this new pulse of human creativity had yet to arrive on the scene. The planners, analysers, think-tankers, policy "wonks", administrators et al. were still creatures of the future. In short, South Africa was a nation of doers. You only earned money if you added measurable value to society. You were entitled to nothing. You worked in order for you and your family to live because there was no state-sponsored welfare – just the churches and a few other charitable institutions.

Now I am not about to say that we have made no progress at all since then. The institutionalisation of society over this century has brought with it certain benefits. Human endeavour, organised in large units, has been responsible for mining projects which individual diggers and prospectors could not in any manner have undertaken. Agriculture, commerce and industry have in a similar way evolved into structures which produce things considerably cheaper in real terms than their predecessors on account of economies of scale. South Africa has developed an infrastructure of roads, bridges, airports, a telecommunication system and an electricity grid which is replicated nowhere else in Africa. Indeed, we are envied by some developed countries as well.

Nevertheless, there has been major retrogression as well. Layer upon layer of nonvalue-adding officialdom has been piled on to the productive base of South Africa. To pay for these layers, taxes by international standards have climbed to unreasonable heights. Reams of red tape stifle any further waves of entrepreneurial energy. We have more conferences per square kilometre than any other country on earth. Rhetoric flows freely, endless plans are made but the deeds don't follow.

Attention is focused on defining people's rights and saying that society must observe them. It is better to encourage a positive climate for business which will naturally create more jobs, thus allowing the job-holders to satisfy the rights for themselves. We have a crisis of delivery in terms of housing, schools, hospitals and all other sorts of good works because communities are not generating the income to afford them. In short, business is playing second fiddle to politics and the outcome is close to paralysis.

Now that the economy is under legitimate management, what an opportunity exists to change the direction of the last 95 years. Let us cut business people loose from the bonds of bureaucracy. Let us produce a constitution which is unabashedly in support of developing our own entrepreneurs and wooing foreign investment to this country. The rush will then be on again. But it won't be for diamonds and gold. This time the gems to be discovered and the veins to be mined will be the talents of ordinary people who want to make a difference to their own quality of life by their own efforts. If managed properly, this resource will never be depleted.

The New Economy

So let's now examine what the New Economy should look like compared to the Old Economy.

2.2.1997 The New Economy. I like it as a catch phrase because it suggests the need for a paradigm shift. And since we already have the New South Africa, it logically follows that the country needs a new, transformed and very different economy.

Let's first examine the Old Economy. Its origin lies with Fleetwood Rawstorne. He was the man, or at least it was his cook Damon, who discovered three small diamonds on Colesberg Kopje on a clear, moonlit night in July 1871. As the plaque erected by the National Monuments Council at the Big Hole says: "This discovery marked the birth of Kimberley. The wealth derived from this and other diamond mines in the area laid the foundation of the industrialisation of South Africa."

That and the double whammy of finding gold on the Witwatersrand ten years later led to the greatest entrepreneurial surge in South Africa's history. This century has really seen the consolidation and institutionalisation of an economy created by the raw, energetic entrepreneurs at the end of the previous one. Most of the major companies in existence here today can trace their roots directly or indirectly to the exploitation of the original diamond and gold fields. Moreover, with the growing sophistication of the Old Economy has gone an astonishing proliferation of political and economic overheads. Three-tier government with three-tier bureaucracies, associations lobbying for this or that cause, bodies that monitor whether business is complying with the ever-widening thicket of laws, rules and regulations – they all have to be paid for out of the basic operating units of the Old Economy. So it is creaking badly.

Somehow the mindset of the Old Economy is out of tune too. We had business heroes in the 1880s. Their names were on everybody's lips. Just think of Rhodes, Barnato, Beit. How many captains of industry today would receive a standing ovation from the crowd at the First National Bank soccer stadium if they decided to do a lap of honour? Politicians and sports stars have displaced the giants of industry in the public's mind.

So what are the pillars of the New Economy? I believe there are seven.

The first is the encouragement of industries which can sustain high profit margins in today's global economy. Inevitably, this means a shift in our economy towards information and services. For example, we should be attracting every conceivable world-class company in these fields to establish a base in South Africa. Secondly, we must go flat out on small business development where the majority of jobs will in future be created. It just so happens that, in this postmodernist age, the greatest opportunities for business start-ups lie in information and services too. Of course, this does not rule out agriculture and manufacturing where ingenious entrepreneurs will find niches.

The third pillar is the mobilisation of risk capital throughout the land. This is the reason I've suggested provincial stock exchanges. They're better than casinos. The fourth pillar is entrepreneurial training in schools, which has to be common sense since matriculants are no longer guaranteed jobs in the formal sector (like they were in the Old Economy of the 1950s). The fifth pillar is the end of overheads. We must zero base every overhead job in this country and discard all those that are adding no value.

The sixth pillar is that this time around the entrepreneurial revolution is broad-based, encompassing blacks and whites, women and men, graduates and squatters. We need an all-inclusive economy. The seventh pillar of the New Economy? Well, we have to develop an all-consuming passion for business in this country – the kind we have for sport. It has to be exciting and adventurous. It must give people self-esteem and dignity. We need the same commitment as the teacher who for no extra money teaches a barefoot Afrikaans kid to become a world-beating Springbok rugby player.

The perfect seven. Why not?

Joblessness

Joblessness is more basic than homelessness. But there's absolutely no excuse for joblessness in a world experiencing an unprecedented economic boom. Bad policies are to blame.

18.6.1995   What do a conversation with a young graduate over supper in Hermanus, a lead article in the *False Bay Echo* and a *Newsweek* interview with economist Jeremy Rifkin have in common? The answer is: a radical change in the job market.

The graduate in question had an exemplary record at Pretoria Boy's High and a Bachelor of Commerce degree from Wits. He has been searching very hard for a job in Cape Town without success since last November. He has followed up every lead provided by advertisements, agencies and friends. Certainly from my brief chat to him, he struck me as having all the qualities necessary to make an excellent prospect for any organisation willing to employ him – a good business sense, a steady temperament, a pleasing disposition, an ambition to get somewhere and the knowledge that you have to work hard to get there. Twenty years ago he would have had difficulties deciding which offer to accept. Now nobody is making him even one offer.

A recurring theme in conversations he's had over finding work is: it's not what you know but whom you know that determines your chances. His experience runs totally counter to all the statistics which we've been led to believe over the years about impending shortages of graduates for management positions in South Africa. Indeed most companies here are thinning their managerial ranks in response to the more competitive environment brought on by South Africa's re-entry into overseas markets. At present, there's a surplus of young managers around, not a deficit. I remember a case recently of a Wits engineering graduate dropping the fact that he had a degree cum laude from his CV in order to get on the first rung of the employment ladder. He landed a job as a draughtsman with a major construction company and was only going to inform them of his degree once he was sure that his services would be retained. This is the very opposite of the previous practice of "embroidering" a CV to get a job. Nowadays a high-sounding CV evokes the response: "Dear Sir, I am afraid you are too qualified to be considered blah, blah, blah . . ."

So the top end of the job market is exceedingly tough. What about the other end? Enter the ongoing controversy surrounding hawking in Fish Hoek's Main Road. This was heightened by a teenager bumping the trestle table of a street trader which caused several ornaments to fall to the pavement and break. The trader demanded compensation whereupon the teenager withdrew R1 000 from his savings account at the bank (he'd earned the money at a local restaurant) and paid the trader. His father is now seeking to have the money returned on the grounds that his son was intimidated by the trader. This incident was described under the headline "Storm over Hawking" in the local newspaper.

The local Residents Association and Chamber of Business are asking the municipality to declare the Main Road a restricted area for hawking and to provide an alternative site. Older members of the community in particular dislike the mess and the nuisance. But the hawkers don't want to move because they naturally want to be where the pedestrian traffic is thickest. But you have to ask: what is creating this stressful situation in the first place?

Here we move on to the prognostications of Mr Rifkin in his book *The End of Work*. He predicts that by the year 2025 only 2 per cent of the world's workforce will be blue-collar factory workers. Already the proportion has dropped from one-third in the 1960s to 17 per cent today. The reason he gives is that "as we move into the Information Age, computers and robots are replacing whole job categories". In addition, "white-collar middle management, secretaries, receptionists are going. Wholesalers are being eliminated as manufacturers deal with retailers directly through electronic interchange."

There you have it. In the Western Cape, graduates are getting a zero response to applications for employment and hawkers are being forced to hawk in places where they are unpopular because of a global phenomenon: joblessness. It is a pity that the RDP laid greater emphasis on housing than on jobs. If a person has a job, he can get a house, but the same does not apply the other way round. Joblessness is more fundamental than homelessness. Solve the former and automatically you're on your way to solving the latter.

Rifkin offers the solution that "every country ought to consider providing an income voucher as an alternative to welfare, for those willing to be trained for meaningful work in the nonprofit sector . . . social skills are the only ones the computer can't take over. Operating a day-care center with 30 kids is too complex for a computer, whereas surgery can be done by robots." That's a thought. I personally believe we have to revisit the concept of villages where people perform simple tasks for one another. Whatever the route out of the current jobless trap, Rifkin has the final word: "People forced out of the market place will take by force what they can't earn."

How to reduce inequity

You will therefore only reduce inequity by creating a new class of entre-preneurs. The alternative scenario is "the lame flamingo" – an economy that is pink and unable to fly.

24.11.1996 I didn't write *The High Road: Where are we now?* to gain favourable critiques or win awards. I wrote it to start a revolution – or to be more exact an entrepreneurial revolution. I believe as pas-sionately as any socialist that we must close the gap between rich and poor. That's why the cover of the book is red! Where I differ is that I do not think the state is the most effective agency to achieve that objective.

Social inequity during this century, despite the best efforts of govern-ments to attack the problem, has proved an extremely hard nut to crack. It has ironically got worse in those countries whose rulers have followed explicit left-wing agendas and better in countries with free-market leanings. The sheer persistence of inequity suggests a lack of social mobility in many societies because people are caught in positive and negative feedback loops.

A positive feedback loop is where children of successful upper-class families in, say, England do well themselves because they have a stimulating environment at home; are educated at the best schools and universities; get the breaks in the job market – especially in the City of London – and marry a spouse out of the same drawer. A negative feedback loop is where a kid from the East End of London has a father who is on the dole; cannot, even with talent, break out of the stultifying impact of indifferent teachers in rundown classrooms; has to contend with friends who regard it as an act of betrayal to move up the ladder; never develops the skills to rise above a menial job and marries into another subachieving family.

It is simply no good pumping money in to sustain disadvantaged people while such social barriers remain in place. It merely creates a dependency on the state and reduces the incentive of the recipients of aid to try and vault the barriers. For instance, in the US and Australia, disadvantaged Indians and Aborigines respectively have been on the receiving end of traditional hand-out policies for years. It has done them no good at all. To the contrary, in fact, it has produced a result which the former proponents of apartheid would have been proud of – separate Indian reserves in America and dilapidated Aboriginal suburbs in Australian cities. No integration at all. Bitterness on all sides.

This is what leads me to declare that South Africa needs a revolution in thinking to deal with the problems of social immobility, segregation and a national income distribution which is perceived to be skewed too much in favour of the rich. If you look at the experience of Hungary, Poland, the Czech Republic, Chile, Argentina, Thailand and Taiwan, they all tell you one thing. The most powerful driving force behind transforming the prospects of the poor and under-privileged and allowing them to break the shackles of impoverishment is small business development. Hungary has so far in 1996 had the hottest stock market in the world in dollar terms for precisely this reason. In Poland there are now two million small and medium-sized enterprises operating, generating 50 per cent of GDP and 60 per cent of employment.

There is still an impression in this country that if you're an entrepreneur running a small business, you are only doing this because you have to. The small and microbusiness sectors are considered a refugee camp for those unlucky enough not to find jobs in the formal sector. However, nothing could be further from the truth. Many people who run their own businesses do not want to work in the formal sector, to be a small fish in a large pond or to have a boss telling them what to do. They consider running a small business as an exciting adventure. They obtain more dignity and self-esteem out of being their own boss.

Developing a new class of entrepreneurs is therefore central to the goal of greater equality in South Africa.

Squatters

But we must change our mindset about squatters because they are the ultimate entrepreneurs. When I addressed an audience in Khayelitsha the other night, it was made clear to me that they are not demanding hand-outs. They want a piece of the action. Someone suggested modifying the stokvel system to become a stock exchange. Instead of each member of the stokvel putting money in every month and scooping the pool once a year, the money put in would be evenly distributed across all the businesses covered by the stokvel. Trading in the shares of these businesses could then begin between the members. Not a bad idea at all. Pursuing this line of thinking, another approach might be to form a Khayelitsha Investment Trust which holds shares in a variety of small businesses there. Institutional investors and members of the public would be invited to buy units in KIT on the basis that the risk is lowered by the diversity of its portfolio. The government might chip in too.

29.12.1996 Having requested Nelson Mandela to provide bobbies on the beat in the New Year, I'm going to be greedy this weekend. I have a wish in another area too, that of creating a new entrepreneurial class in South Africa. This, however, cannot be done by the State President, the government or big business alone. Unlike the political transition which needed the combined wisdom of a handful of political leaders, the birth of an entrepreneurial class requires a grassroots revolution – a change in the national mindset.

To show the magnitude of the change needed, think of a squatter. Most people in the formal sector regard him/her as a liability rather than an asset. Squatters in the neighbourhood raise the incidence of theft, so the better-off declare. Put them anywhere but not in my backyard. However, to me the squatter is the ultimate form of entrepreneur for the simplest of reasons: he/she is closest to the edge of survival. If I were plonked in the middle of nowhere – on a rocky knoll or a shifting sand dune – or squeezed into a vacant urban lot between high-rise office towers and told "go find yourself some shelter and make some money on the side", I wouldn't have a clue what to do. I've had support systems all my life, whether it be a caring family, a good education, working for a big corporation or enough savings to get me out of trouble. From the day I was born, I've never had nothing. Rather, the receipt of pocket money as a child taught me that parents are the welfare state, and socialism is the best deal!

Squatters, on the other hand, presume that nothing is going to be provided by the state. They're on their own and they'll do the best they can. They therefore use innovative means to gather materials unofficially for their shacks. Most shacks do the job of being a home despite their patched-up appearance on the outside. Indeed, I saw a photograph in a newspaper the other day of a double-storey one erected by an enterprising individual. But what changed my mind about squatters were comments made to me by members of a community outside Welkom when Joe Slovo and I were attending the launch of an RDP housing project.

"Clem, do you really feel I should take on a mortgage loan in addition to the government grant in order to buy one of these houses?" asked one. "I won't be able to pay the interest out of my subsistence earnings," said another. Hardly the observations of irresponsible parasitic human beings, I thought.

What squatters want most are jobs, not houses. They represent a constituency which is much larger than Cosatu's membership. They are the majority of the ANC's political base. They are not going to be absorbed by the civil service since the government is attempting to cut its budget deficit by removing 100 000 people from its workforce. They are not going to be employed in sufficient numbers by big business which, for reasons of global competitiveness, is necessarily capital-intensive. *Quod erat demonstrandum* – they have to become self-employed entrepreneurs or work in small agricultural, manu-facturing or service-oriented enterprises.

In the next three years, it will be nice to grow our economy at 6 per cent per annum, expand our export earnings, raise investment as a share of GDP and have the government balance its books. But it will be more of an accomplishment if we can take the squatter community and provide an environment which enables them to improve their own lot and thereby purchase houses without the assistance of the RDP. Narrowing the Gini coefficient – or the gap between the haves and the have-nots – will also allow the ANC to sleep in their beds at night in the lead-up to the next election.

With this objective in mind, perhaps an economic Codesa is appropriate, where the small entrepreneurs are well represented.

Economic Codesa

An economic Codesa is no bad thing with small business well represented. It should talk in the first place about business creation as this will lead to job creation. It should also address Whag – What happens after gold?

5.1.1997 If an economic Codesa were to be held, what type of agenda should it follow? My recommendation would be to design an agenda which produces a highly specific programme of action with deadlines, accountable individuals for each task and a series of follow-up meetings of a small executive to monitor progress. The grand objective is to create an environment friendly for small entrepreneurs. I've chosen these words carefully since you can't plan an increase in entrepreneurs. That's a contradiction in terms. You can merely create a favourable set of initial conditions and hope that it leads to a self-sustaining chain reaction.

Let's start with an analogy which divides the agenda neatly into three parts. If government's macroeconomic strategy is the launch pad for growth, entrepreneurs are the rocket and venture capital is the rocket fuel. The rocket scientists are the guys who've done it already – turned their initial concepts into successful businesses today. Their advice will be invaluable.

Topics which examine the best sort of launch pad could include a possible corporate tax holiday for businesses up to a certain size. Not only is one trying to give the most alluring incentive for people to plunge into the entrepreneurial sea, but the cost of collecting taxes effectively for microbusinesses probably outweighs the potential revenue to be raised. Italy demonstrates how easily small business owners can hoodwink snooping tax inspectors with a second set of books. First-time entrepreneurs who do not pay corporate tax will still be contributing to state coffers through paying VAT. As for the idea that larger businesses will divide themselves up into a myriad of microbusinesses to escape tax, one simply closes this loophole with legislation and criminal penalties. Obviously, the other area of focus must be the reasonable removal of all regulations currently inhibiting entrepreneurial development. I say "reasonable" because there are basic conditions of health, safety, environmental protection and legality of business which must be met. But that should be it.

On the second element, the rocket, the issue of entrepreneurial training in every school curriculum and such training being universally available to adults should be effectively aired. In addition, big business and government (at national, provincial and municipal levels) should agree on outsourcing as many of their activities as possible to stimulate microbusinesses. Anglo's Small Business Unit shows that it can be done. We're up to contracts worth R250 million a year. Gauteng municipalities have also been enterprising in dividing up the function of waste collection so that individual entrepreneurs can lease trucks to cover particular streets. This also has the benefit of closing the loop of accountability. People know exactly who is responsible if their rubbish is not collected. That person can lose the contract for malperformance. Stutterheim should be studied as a small town that was on the brink of disaster because of the droughts in the Eastern Cape but which has made a remarkable comeback through fostering small enterprise. Perhaps a chair of small enterprise needs to be established at one of the universities so that serious research can be properly undertaken in the whole field.

The third element is the rocket fuel. A genuine over-the-counter stock market should be explored. In the US, Nasdaq attracts a huge amount of IPOs (initial public offerings) and trades similar daily volumes of shares as the New York Stock Exchange. Here the cost of issuing a prospectus is prohibitive for a small entrepreneur seeking capital from the market. Somehow, we have to return to the energetic Johannesburg of the 1880s when a prospector waved his claim in front of a group of strangers and offered them a share in any gold strike in return for their money. One scrap of paper sealed the deal. Today, red tape effectively blocks such a transaction. On the microlending side, greater support by the banking industry of existing agencies such as Get Ahead, Triple Trust, the Start-Up Fund and stokvels should be debated.

These are just preliminary ideas which must be fleshed out by the parties concerned. But I hope I've whetted your appetite.

Female entrepreneurs

And don't forget that women are an important economic force. In some countries, they make the best entrepreneurs. For those parents who argue that they don't send their daughters to school to be turned into greedy little capitalists, I have the following response. Either they become greedy little capitalists or the chances are that they will be a permanent drain on the family finances until they get married.

12.5.1996 It's official. Women are cleverer than men. A recent survey among minority groups in America showed that women outclass men at school and university and progress to higher positions in business and law. In terms of national examination results in England, twenty of the top thirty schools are girls-only schools including St Paul's Girls School in London which holds number one position.

I knew this fact a long time ago. I went up to Oxford with my cousin in 1963. I managed to gain a place at New College. She won a scholarship to Somerville. I got a second in Politics, Philosophy and Economics. She got a first. But the really humiliating aspect of the whole experience was that she was fourteen when she won the scholarship and seventeen when she graduated. It's something I've had to recognise – the women in my family are smarter than the men.

In Bangladesh, there's a bank which makes small loans to the rural poor. It is called the Grameen Bank. Six years after beginning the bank, its founder, Mohammed Yunus, was struck by a particular trend among his borrowers. Women were using the money to better effect than men. They were using profits to build their businesses and improve the quality of life of their families whereas men dissipated the money on entertaining themselves. He decided to concentrate on attracting women to be the bank's customers. Despite a backlash from traditionalists who believe he is undermining the authority conferred upon the husband by society, he has succeeded beyond his most optimistic expectations. Nearly all of his two million borrowers are now women. Having staked their claim to be the best small entrepreneurs in Bangladesh, women are asserting themselves in other spheres such as local politics. Talk about empowerment. This is it.

In Britain, indications are that more women are establishing first-time

89

businesses that are surviving over the long haul than men. Dare I suggest the reason why? Perhaps it's because women are generally more sensitive than their male counterparts to the emotions and thoughts of others. Hence, they relate to customers better and are more flexible in adapting to changes in consumer tastes and values. When inspired by a commercial objective, women often show greater determination and perseverance in meeting it because they know the odds are stacked against them in a man's world. Finally, entrepreneurs tend to be more right-side-of-the-brain oriented which elevates lateral thinking over analytical prowess. Women can often have leaps of intuition which leave menfolk scratching their heads!

Certainly in South Africa the best entrepreneurship training programmes that I've come across are at girls' schools – like the Wykeham Collegiate in Pietermaritzburg and St Mary's DSG in Kloof. Besides being encouraged to try their hand at being entrepreneurs, the girls learn generally how to become enterprising individuals who can contribute to the wellbeing of the community. Would that all schools in South Africa followed their example.

However, the biggest lesson of all to any budding entrepreneur is that a "cross" does not mean "wrong". It means "try again". In Japan, the average entrepreneur only gets it right after opening up the sixth or seventh business. The previous failures were all used to climb the learning curve. Maybe that's why South African women will predominate in the new entrepreneurial class. They are more willing to learn from their mistakes than their male counterparts and bounce back from adversity.

Local stock markets

There is a good old Texas saying: "Big hat, no cattle", i.e. without money an idea lacks substance. Capitalism was so called to emphasise that capital makes business go round. It rests on two foundations: the limited liability company where you can only lose the stake you put into the company (unlike Lloyd's where you can lose your shirt) and a stock exchange where entrepreneurs can raise capital from strangers. For cynics who believe a local stock exchange is too small to be viable, think of the Casablanca, Nairobi, Lusaka and Windhoek exchanges. They're thriving. On account of the latest technologies which permit screen-based trading through local area networks of personal computers, transaction costs can be reduced to a minimum. Anyway, stock exchanges are better than casinos for satisfying the national gambling instinct. Those who took the risk and invested in companies created by Sir Ernest Oppenheimer, Anton Rupert and Donald Gordon did a great deal better that those who lent them money. A worry is that without proper controls, scams will happen. But "caveat emptor" has always applied, the most recent example being Bre-X which went from zero to $3 billion and back to zero when it was discovered the gold in Indonesia wasn't there (a case of the golden fleece). In fact, the establishment of exchanges specialising in penny stocks could be the catalyst which makes the entrepreneurial revolution happen here. Ironically, the unions would understand this because they now have investment companies well versed in the game of buying and selling shares. The success of the "personal finance" supplements in the national newspapers also bears witness to the potential interest of the public in such a development.

19.1.1997   Over the last six months or so, we've all been waiting with bated breath to see which consortia are going to get casino licences in each province. Although I don't gamble myself except for small flutters on the golf course and bridge table, I'm not opposed to casinos popping up around the place. I doubt, though, that they will be as lucrative as the one at Sun City simply because there will be so many more of them. Competition will take its toll on profit margins and the market will be fragmented.

I can't say that I'm overenthusiastic about a proliferation of casinos either. Whatever people say, personal and even family lives will be ruined as unscrupulous loan sharks take the opportunity of bailing out addicted losers. Heavies will lurk in the background to enforce repayment of debt. The underground is never far away from the sheen on the surface. On the other hand, you can't go too far in the direction of protecting people from themselves. As in the case of alcohol, libertarians will advise that you should leave private citizens to their own (de)vices as long as they're not harming anybody else. And on the positive side, plenty of new jobs will be created by the casinos. Moreover, the additional tax and licence fees they pay can be devoted to welfare.

However, I have one reservation. Casinos per se are not associated with the process of wealth creation. In fact, quite the reverse. The operators have figured out the odds in each game to ensure that customers are parted from their wealth in the long run. At best, it's zero sum. What you lose, the house gains. At worst, slots are a voluntary tax on the poor. So let's be original. I believe there is a much more beneficial way of satisfying the nation's gambling instinct which is clearly evident from the success of scratch card and similar operations.

Why don't we have local stock exchanges – say a Durban one as well as others based in Cape Town, Port Elizabeth, Bloemfontein, Nelspruit, etc? These would be focused on providing equity capital for small business ventures in their respective provinces. Local stockbrokers would match local entrepreneurs needing finance with local institutions and members of the public who were prepared to take bets in the venture capital field. For example, a Natal firm keen on expanding its manufactured exports from the port of Durban to India and the Far East could list itself on the Durban Exchange. A Western Cape family wanting some immediate cash could float part of its wine farm on the Cape Town Exchange. The possibilities are endless and of course there would be nothing to stop a local exchange seeking investors from across the provincial border.

It would in addition put the financing of small business on a far more sensible footing. Borrowing 100 per cent of the capital to open up a first-time business is a mug's game. Interest and loan repayments are certain, profit is not. Much better to share the upside potential and downside risk with other shareholders. That's what the original pioneers did with the diamond and gold mines.

You might claim that the Johannesburg Stock Exchange can do all this already perfectly well. Moreover, local stock exchanges are rare overseas. If the idea was that good, there'd be plenty of them. On the first count, the JSE is where it is because that was where the gold was. It should be congratulated for subsequently using this accidental geological windfall to good effect to become the nation's prime provider of equity capital. However, it lacks the local knowledge which is so essential for dabbling in small-enterprise stocks. As our economy becomes more diverse both functionally and geographically, does it make sense to have just one stock exchange to mobilise the nation's capital? A compromise might be to establish local branches of the JSE (or franchises) on the grounds that it is not sensible to reinvent the wheel completely. Perhaps they can come up with simplified procedures to reduce the cost of floating a new company below the current figure of R500 000.

Alternatively, NASDAQ – the American Stock Exchange specialising in initial public offerings – could tender for management of one of the stock exchanges. Having seen what NASDAQ has done to ginger up the New York Stock Exchange through competition, maybe a little dose here could be worthwhile too. The Australian stock exchange has chosen the Internet as a tool for bringing together small enterprises and investors, by introducing a revolutionary market site. Why not?

The second reservation about the newness of the concept can be easily dealt with. If the economic transformation of South Africa is to be successfully implemented, we have to have some "firsts". Maybe this is one of them. Let's gamble on it!

The Start-up Fund

However, if you would prefer to borrow the money, here's how The Start-Up Fund works. Normal banks are understandably cautious about lending directly to microbusiness because it's not their money they're lending – it's yours. If you walked up to the teller and asked to withdraw R100 from your account and she said, "The manager blew it last week on a loan to a microbusiness", you wouldn't be impressed. This does not, however, exclude banks from using specialist agencies like the Start-up Fund as a conduit for loans to small business. Furthermore, were the usury law to be scrapped, a market-related interest rate would encourage greater direct lending as well.

21.4.1996　As a columnist, it's nice once in a while to have a scoop. This one concerns the Start-Up Fund. I can do nothing better than quote the invitation to its first press conference: "Using sophisticated technology, the Start-Up Fund successfully serves the 'untouchables' of the banking sector – providing loan capital to unemployed people in the informal sector starting up in business. To general amazement, the Start-Up Fund has emerged as a viable financial institution serving thousands of microentrepreneurs throughout South Africa – covering all its costs from its own earnings, with zero bad-debt impact. *Incredible? Yes, but true!*"

To those of cynical persuasion, this may sound like yet another over-hyped scheme where the promises are empty. But when I mention that the capital to start the SUF was supplied by the Development Bank of Southern Africa, the Independent Development Trust, the Anglo American and De Beers Chairman's Fund, Metropolitan Life, the Nedcor Community Development Fund, Southern Life, JCI, First National Bank, the Foschini Group and the Industrial Development Corporation, it should persuade anybody that this initiative has substance. It has also been warmly endorsed by the office of the State President.

The SUF is the brainchild of Tony Davenport. A graduate of Rhodes University, he is a marvellous hybrid – an accountant with a higher sense of calling. After working as an economist at Assocom and doing a stint as a financial journalist, he switched to running a farm and being a missionary in Matabeleland, Zimbabwe. In 1985, he settled in Cape Town where he founded the Triple Trust and the Informal Business Training

Trust. These two institutions have provided a highly effective ladder of opportunity for unemployed people to become self-employed in microbusiness. IBTT has trained over 20 000 emerging entrepreneurs with outstanding results. For example, a recent survey showed that 81 per cent of unemployed people at the Orange Farm township had become economically active since completing the IBTT programme. No wonder that the course is affectionately called the "Township MBA".

So Tony has an excellent track record. But how does the SUF work? Despite being a nonprofit organisation, the way loans are granted has been thought through in a very hard-headed way. As an applicant, you need to do three things: put down R75 in cash as a refundable deposit; go through a microenterprise training course provided by one of 75 designated organisations (eg: IBTT, STRIVE Foundation, the School Leavers Opportunity Trust, the Association for Micro-Enterprise Business Activity, the National Union of Mineworkers); and open a bank account.

You then receive your first advance of R250 for three months. At the same time your loan account is debited with an additional sum of R50 which is credited to the Group Indemnity Trust (along with your initial deposit of R75). The GIT is a separate trust which provides group surety to the SUF on behalf of all borrowers. If any bad debts are incurred by defaulting borrowers, the SUF is compensated by the GIT. The GIT also provides life and funeral insurance to the borrowers. Moreover, in the event of a surplus in the GIT at the end of each year after settlement of insurance claims and bad debts, bonuses are paid to the borrowers who are up to date with their repayments.

In return for the R250 loan, you have to repay R120 per month for three months, R360 in total. That sounds a lot. However, the R110 surplus not only covers the GIT debit of R50, it also pays for the cost of money lent to the SUF, the computer equipment, deposit books, bank charges, printing costs, tax and phone bills, postage and stationery, office rent and salaries of the SUF (one full-time employee with a personal computer and one computer consultant). Providing you make your repayment in full and on time, you can enter the second phase of borrowing R500 for six months. Thereafter, at six monthly intervals, you can move to R750, R1 000, R1 500 and R2 000. The incentive to repay in each phase is strong because you can borrow

95

more money next time round up to a maximum of R2 000. All transactions are handled through First National Bank's network. Your deposit book has a code number which allows your repayment to be immediately picked up in the SUF data base, no matter which branch you pay from.

The SUF commenced operating on 1 October 1993. It now occupies a critical niche in South Africa's capital markets. There are at present 3 500 borrowers with total loans of around R3 million. The base is still small but the model has proven itself – and the potential for expansion is enormous.

Dollar-based economy
What about a dollar-based economy in South Africa? The relaxation on 1 July 1997 is a good start.

1.12.1996 One of the points made in *The High Road: Where are we now?* is that the movement of skilled people and capital around the world is becoming increasingly free. The abolition of exchange controls by South Africa would be in step with this trend.

A more radical scenario would be that South Africa becomes a dual exchange economy. People could exchange products and services within South Africa by paying in either rands or dollars. They could hold their savings here in either currency too. This would in some ways parallel Europe's move towards monetary union in 1999. The euro is scheduled to replace Europe's individual currencies completely, but there may well be a period of transition during which the euro is used alongside each domestic currency. Of course, the major difference is that the euro is an entirely new nonnationalistic currency, whereas the dollar is the traditional currency of the United States.

Before such a scenario is dismissed out of hand on the grounds that the South African government will lose monetary control or exporters will no longer gain the benefits of a depreciating rand (a temporary gain anyway), think about the upsides. One of the main fears is that when exchange controls are lifted, South African citizens will move their savings en masse offshore and drive the rand down to new lows. The advantage of allowing residents to hold dollars inside South Africa is that to a large extent the stampede could be averted – as long as the permanence of such a concession was believed. Moreover, it would certainly be better than the present position of skilled people having to emigrate overseas in order to accumulate hard currency savings.

You can also bet that as dollars become more freely available in the local economy, hotels, shops and restaurants would increasingly quote their prices and ask for payment in dollars. Workers might demand the same too. In effect, we would gradually move from a dual-based to a dollar-based economy. Is that such a bad thing? We would suddenly be able to benchmark the domestic prices of goods and labour against those of any other economy in the world. We would have a much more direct measurement of our international competitiveness than we do now with a fluctuating rand. This in turn would put pressure on us to reduce our inflation rate to the 2-3 per cent level prevailing in advanced economies, and to grant salary and wage increases linked more closely to improvements in performance and productivity.

For foreigners, our economy and the accounts of our companies would be easier to interpret if all the data were to be in dollars. In addition, foreigners would no longer have to contend with the risks of making profitable returns on their South African investments in rands, only to see them vanish when they convert their depreciating rands back into dollars. In monetary terms, we would become an extension of the United States. Perhaps we could join the North American Free Trading Area as well. That would give our exporters a boost.

All this makes one think, doesn't it? But that's what scenarios are supposed to do!

Trust

Trust between strangers is essential for a world-class economy to operate. Another obvious attribute is the ability to communicate not only locally but internationally as well. By the year 2000 it is estimated that $1\frac{1}{2}$ billion people – a quarter of the world's population – will speak English either as a first or second language. English is increasingly the language of choice in business, science and entertainment. Around 75 per cent of the world's mail is currently written in English as is around 80 per cent of the electronic mail on the Internet. Globalisation applies to tongues as well as economies.

14.1.1996 There I was, on a Sunday morning recently, sitting in the Osteria restaurant overlooking Cottesloe Beach in Perth, Western Australia. I asked a young waitress called Kim for a banana milk shake. She came back to my table after a few minutes to say that she had no ice cream, normally a vital constituent of this delectable concoction. "But," Kim said, "I have some frozen bananas in the fridge which I can crush and add to the milk so that the result is just as good." I asked Kim how she knew. "Trust me," she responded. Sure enough, she returned with an ice-cold banana milk shake which was scintillating.

This brought to mind Francis Fukuyama's latest book called *Trust: Social Virtues and the Creation of Prosperity*. In it he argues that the principal driving force behind economically successful societies is trust. Strangers have to trust one another to work together in large-scale enterprises and to make deals with one another. For example, "My word is my bond" has always been a cornerstone of London's stock market. But it goes deeper than business and the creation of wealth, because trust comes into play in virtually every aspect of society.

The reason is simple. The choices behind any decision you make in the real world are never logically obvious. Only in mathematics do you have answers of the "two plus two equals four" variety. Where there is any uncertainty, rational analysis only gets you so far. Thereafter you're operating on instinct, hunch, gut-feel – call it what you will. When people are involved, we call it trust. Faith is an alternative description but this is usually applied in a religious context.

So let's see just how universal trust has to be in order for society to be viable. When you board an aircraft, you're trusting in the integrity of the airline and particularly in the competence of the pilots who fly the plane and of the engineers who service it. If you go into hospital, you unquestioningly accept the skills of the doctors and nurses. When you send a letter, you are trusting that it will arrive within a few days. Nobody is going to open it on the way. As a driver, you trust that the car coming towards you will stay in the correct lane.

When you get married, you trust that your partner will be faithful. As you send your children to school, you are trusting in the good characters of the principal and the teachers. They will protect your kids from harm. If you're a Matric student, you trust in the honesty and ability of the people who mark your examination papers. They will deliver an objective judgement of your efforts.

While you walk the dogs in the park, you trust that other pedestrians are not about to mug you. When you visit the shops, you more than hope that the shopkeepers are not ripping you off. You assume the vegetables are fresh (though you may inspect them), the yoghurt sell-by dates are genuine, the household appliances work or you can take them back, the brand names on the clothes are real, the medicine has not been tampered with and the wine is not watered down. Reading the newspaper in the morning, you expect the advertisements to be passably accurate and the news to approximate the truth.

So trust is central to civilisation and progress. Lose it and we will all become suspicious and inward-looking. And that spells retrogression. Self-reliance is terribly limiting. At times, we have to trust a stranger.

Decentralised bargaining
Decentralised bargaining and a flexible labour market are equally essential.

20.8.1995   In the field of industrial relations, centralised bargaining has been a dominant issue here in recent months. It was therefore with much interest that I read the following paragraphs in a recent edition of *The Economist*. They referred to the present state of play in Britain.

"Even where bargaining is still collective, it happens down the line.

The multi-employer national agreements that used to determine private-sector wages have collapsed – in engineering, banking, cotton textiles, food retailing, cement and newspapers, for example. In every case, according to David Metcalf, professor of industrial relations at the London School of Economics, the change has been initiated by management and opposed by the unions.

"In 1990, the authoritative Workplace Industrial Relations Survey, carried out by a group of academics, showed that, of every five workers on whose behalf collective bargaining still took place, only one was covered by a national deal. Four were covered by deals for each individual firm. Even company-wide bargaining is breaking down as firms settle pay and conditions at the workplace level, or for particular groups of employees within each workplace."

This isn't surprising. One of the global trends that emerged in the 1960s and has strengthened ever since then is the decentralisation of power in society. Partially it's a result of individuals placing higher value on self-expression and personal autonomy which goes with rising educational standards. Partially it's because of the collapse of centrally planned economies and large monolithic companies. Organisations of every kind are becoming flatter, looser-knit and more flexible in the face of change. Partially it's due to modern technology which has empowered ordinary citizens in their relationship to the state. Information grants power. The universal presence of the press, radio and television, personal computers and the Internet gives families everywhere the data on which to make up their own minds about prevailing issues. Ignorance may be bliss but it's also a sign of weakness. There's less ignorance around these days and more independence of thought.

Centralised bargaining is simply the victim of this general trend of giving more power to the people. Workers want more say in negotiating their own conditions in their own companies and in their own workplaces. That's what worker participation means. They are less willing to allow their lives to be determined by remote national negotiating teams, however well intentioned and skilful they are in the art of extracting maximum concessions from employers. Local union branches and local shop stewards are demanding more say in union affairs from the national leadership. After all, unions are not immune from decentralisation themselves.

100

Added to all this is the fact that companies in a specific industry are experiencing an ever wider variety of market conditions depending on their locality, their product range and their quality of management. Each company wants to tailor its remuneration systems to its particular circumstances, particularly as the latter can change so fast.

If Britain as a relatively well-unionised economy has moved away from centralised bargaining, it's a fairly safe bet to say that South Africa will do the same. This will place more emphasis on companies having their own in-house negotiating structures incorporating local union representatives. At the same time, there will be less frequent resort to industry-wide forums. In other words, two-tier bargaining is inevitable.

Interprovincial competition

We need some interprovincial competition and a Premier Cup for the province that comes closest to being world class.

2.4.1995 Mention the words "interprovincial competition". One immediately thinks of sport. But it's going to change. As the New South Africa develops, people will perceive differences in the quality of life experienced in the various provinces. In fact, the behaviour of property values is beginning to reflect the realities of each province. Such differences will become a major factor in the final decision of local and overseas industrialists who are wondering where to locate new plants and offices. They might even induce business people to relocate their present operations from one province to another. In these days of microelectronics, where head offices can be set up virtually anywhere complete with fax machine, video-conferencing facilities and cellulars, business is very mobile.

If I were therefore a premier of a province, I would be getting my advisers to draw up a checklist of the important factors in attracting investment and young entrepreneurs, together with their families, to my patch. I would then set about diminishing the unattractive features as identified, and accentuating the strengths. I would also embark on a major promotion campaign to let it be known that the province was open for business.

Up till now, provinces and cities have mainly advertised themselves to increase the number of tourists visiting them. Although tourism creates jobs, it's usually seasonal and economies that rely too much on it are of the boom-and-bust kind. Conditions out of season are pretty grim. Much better to go for the permanency of industrial belts and commercial centres, and to diversify into a range of activities. When one industry is down, the other is up.

Every province is reeling under tremendous unemployment. The most effective way to alleviate this is to gather as many bright-eyed and imaginative entrepreneurs as possible from around the country and overseas under the provincial umbrella and to let them do their own thing. They will hire one or two employees to begin with. The successful ones will expand their workforces into hundreds or thousands. The multiplier effect of these entrepreneurs and their families (as well as their employees and their families) spending money in the provincial economy will add even more jobs. Indeed, with luck, one might achieve a critical mass of activity in one or two sectors such that further business in those sectors naturally gravitates to the province. This has happened in India where certain states have become renowned for diamond cutting while others have focused on the development of computer software.

What would be the factors that I would expect to see included on the checklist? A comparatively low crime rate, good primary and secondary schooling, medical care of a high standard, motivated and productive labour, an unpolluted environment, steady water supplies, well-maintained roads, ready access to an international airport, round-the-clock telecommunication services, decent offices, a friendly central business district, nice suburbs, reasonable rates, rising property values, adequate sport and recreation facilities and above all provincial and local government officials who understand the requirements of business people and positively encourage them to start new ventures in their constituencies.

If readers of this article think that I am sounding unrealistic, then it shows just how much the attitudes of politicians and civil servants in the various provinces are going to have to change. Healthy rivalry between the provinces is the key to obtaining a general improvement in conditions for doing business in this country as a whole.

The provinces that act as pathfinders in implementing business-friendly strategies are likely to be the ones that get the cream of the entrepreneurial crop. We have had the Currie Cup and Castle Cup in sport. What about the Premier Cup for the province that achieves the highest economic growth rate each year or manages to create the most new jobs within its borders? It's about time we had some measurable yardsticks by which to judge the relative performance of politicians on an annual basis. To make it even more interesting, the remuneration of each provincial legislature should be linked to the annual results of that province and the change in its position in the national league. That would be something for the newspapers and financial journals to write about!

KwaZulu-Natal

Perhaps KwaZulu-Natal will show the other provinces the way.

9.2.1997 Action! That's what the director says as the stagehand snaps the clapperboard shut at the start of shooting a movie scene. Little Sister, the Johannesburg two-girl rock 'n roll band, used to spell it out even more graphically: A-C-T-I-O-N.

And so last weekend, it came as no surprise that the political and business leaders who attended the workshop to discuss KwaZulu-Natal's possible futures chose action as the theme. Indeed, it is the pivotal difference between the two scenarios depicted for KZN: "Sukuma, the Winning Team" and "The Mango Tree".

In the first scenario, Sukuma means "arise and do it" in Zulu. Words are translated into action by a disciplined and trained team where all the players are valued for their individual contribution. Based on the building of partnerships (government, business, labour and communities), a three-fold vision for KZN is implemented at unprecedented speed: the spreading of a new entrepreneurial culture to all levels of society; the enhancement of Durban and Richards Bay as two of Africa's leading ports; and the realisation of the potential of KZN as a world-class tourist destination.

By contrast, in the second scenario, very little is done to reap the benefit of KZN's undoubted assets. Fruit occasionally falls from the

103

mango tree into the open mouths of those passively reclining in the shade of the tree. But nobody makes any effort to help the tree grow and provide more fruit.

The scenarios reflect how paralysed we have been up to now to do anything in the New South Africa. Everyone is exasperated but no one makes the first move. The action-prone Americans often joke that their style is "ready, fire, apologise" but it has to be better than ours of "ready, aim, aim, aim . . ." It's as if we have become so obsessed about debating which pistol to use, what kind of bullet, the trajectory to the target, etc. that nobody ever pulls the gun out of the holster, let alone squeezes the trigger. Unless, of course, it's to commit a crime or settle a political score.

I'm glad to say that this time it is going to be different. The KZN workshop put forward a recommended list of priority actions for discussion with other key stakeholders, including a provincial code of conduct, a ports initiative, curriculum reform at schools to promote an entrepreneurial culture and maybe the twinning of Durban with a prominent port city in the East. My favourite, to investigate the establishment of a local stock exchange, featured in the list too.

Ho hum, you may say, just another round of feel-good statements. However, the participants also agreed to a full-time task team being put in place to ensure that marked progress is made in six months. A remarkable young woman who attended the meeting, Vivienne McMenamin, has been proposed as the coordinator of the team. She is, to use a French adjective, *formidable*. Her main wish in life is to make a difference. If anyone call pull KZN's collective trigger in a peaceful way, she can. Action!

Sharp image

Cities have to have a sharp image to draw the crowds. "California Dreaming" could become a reality for SA if LA is twinned with Johannesburg. Around 52 per cent of employment in California is in firms of less than 100 people. California also accounts for a quarter of America's gazelles – companies that double in size in five years – with only 12 per cent of the US population. It is the rainbow state!

31.8.1997 "World class" is an epithet that is applied to cities as well as companies. And just like companies, one of the key attributes is differentiation. Each world-class city has a distinctive character, one that is unique to it. When people go there, they know what to expect.

A significant part of a city's image naturally reflects the prevailing national culture. Whether it's London, Paris, Rome or Beijing, each capital evokes the soul of its respective nation. Nevertheless, quarters within cities may be better known for the subnational group that has chosen to congregate there. Plenty of Chinatowns exist outside China.

Architecture too is an important source of differentiation. The Statue of Liberty in New York, Buckingham Palace in London, The Arc de Triomphe in Paris, St Peter's in Rome – they're all good for the tourist business. Museums, art galleries and opera houses provide themes which reflect the history of the country in which they are situated. There's no way that one city can copycat another city in that respect.

Sometimes, it's natural features that make a city different. Geneva has its lake, Cape Town its mountain and London its river. Sometimes they're man-made green spaces like Central Park in New York and Kensington Gardens in London. One thing's for sure – nobody goes to the centre of any town to see the skyscrapers and offices unless they're on business. Unless it is given special attention, every CBD looks the same.

One other distinctive feature is function. New York with Wall

Street is a financial centre, Canberra with parliament a government centre, Boston with Harvard a learning centre, Detroit with cars a manufacturing centre, New Orleans with jazz a cultural centre and Las Vegas with casinos a gambling centre. In this regard, a world-class city has the ability to attract talented people of a particular genre – a concept called "clustering". Folk singers like Bob Dylan came out of Greenwich Village in New York, while country-and-western musicians head for Memphis and Nashville. For a long time, artists have flocked to Florence and the Latin quarter of Paris.

Silicon Valley is not a city but it attracts some of the most creative intellects in the computer industry. Indeed, California is a role model for South Africa. By itself, the state is one of the top ten economies of the world. But the extraordinary manner in which it has managed to diversify out of defence – previously the main employer in the state – into a wide variety of other industries is a pattern for us to follow as we move away from a mineral-based economy. Los Angeles now has the largest clothes and textile industry in the US, employing 100 000 people and generating annual sales in excess of $10 billion. Next to the garment district is Toytown which produces about 60 per cent of the $12 billion-worth of toys sold in the US and as much again for the overseas market. Multimedia firms in the LA area provide 133 000 jobs as well. And don't forget Hollywood.

LA is really world class and made so by its entrepreneurial spirit and venture capital plus the rainbow quality of its people. I would love to see LA twinned with Johannesburg. What better combination than the city of angels alongside the city of gold!

CBD precincts
If we want to restore our CBDs, divide them up into precincts.

26.1.1997 Precinct. To me, the word suggests a police district in New York. I think of NYPD cars with their sirens wailing, their radios conveying unintelligible messages in short-hand police code and their tyres screeching as they negotiate corners (only just) in pursuit of the wanted.

Now, an American consultant called Richard Bradley has added a new dimension to the word. He has successfully turned around the CBDs of several major American cities including Baltimore and Denver. They were on the skids, the people who worked in businesses located there were desperate, suburbanites believed that the situation was beyond redemption and the exodus out of town was immense. Heard all that before? Well, Bradley changed the paradigm and breathed new life into the heart of these urban jungles.

How so? Bradley suggested to the municipal authorities that their cities should be divided up into a grid of business improvement districts or precincts. The major corporate tenants in each precinct would cough up additional money over and above their rates to remove the crime and grime. But apart from that, they would make their precincts exciting. The CBD as a whole or each precinct within a CBD, if it was really large, would have a theme to attract the public back into town in the evening. Bradley realised that merely having a safe and clean, but sterile and silent, environment was a nonstarter. The CBD had to have an appealing character; a strong image in the mind of suburbanites so that if they travelled there, they would have a different and upbeat emotional experience (not the negative one of being mugged). This is exactly the principle that propels the American masses to Disneyland. You know what you're going to get when you go through their gates. On the other side of the world, "Tel Aviv never goes to sleep" is the motto of Israel's most dynamic city. Even at one in the morning, the streets are still crowded with young revellers.

If we want to revive South African CBDs, they're going to have to swing. They'll have to make young people feel truly cosmopolitan and part of the New South Africa. The Market Theatre area in Johannesburg did exactly that for a time in the 70s and 80s. People descended on the place not so much to watch the latest "struggle" play or listen to township jazz as to get away from apartheid and feel integrated. It was a way of being reborn. The Waterfronts in Cape Town and Randburg have now taken up the running.

Hence, more than business hangs on the future of our CBDs. If we surrender to the polarising tendencies around today, we are spiritually returning to apartheid. I work in the centre of Johannesburg. I occasionally walk uptown for a cappuccino and absorb the atmosphere of the streets. It's so different to the malls of the north.

Despite the CBD's vertical architecture, it's Africa. It's not a hot Surrey like Sandton. So how do we turn public misconceptions about the CBD on their head?

The answer is to go the Bradley route of dividing it up into precincts with identifiable themes – streetside cafés for the young, theatres for the cultural aficionados, an arena for the sports fans. Some will be mixed residential/office areas, a combination of Bohemia and Wall Street. Some will be purely retail but with a special niche to attract customers, like the Oriental Plaza. Some will be cheek-by-jowl market stalls, flea or vegetable. Each precinct will have its cluster of interesting features giving it a name. If Times Square in New York can do it, we can do it too.

London in May

Maybe I'm biased because I was brought up in London, but to me it's a world-class city.

11.6.1995 "We're having a heatwave, a tropical heatwave." As I hummed this old melody, the temperature was close to the worst that February can offer in Pietermaritzburg. But I was in London or more specifically Kensington Gardens. And there were compensations for the heat. Young girls swished past me on roller blades in colourful tank tops and denim shorts. It was a month ago, the first time I'd paid a May visit to London since 1975. I'd forgotten how brilliantly light green are the spring leaves of the weeping beech and lime; how large are the white and pink candelabra-shaped flowers of the horse chestnuts; how infinitely slowly twilight turns into dusk; and how oppressive the climate of the Thames Basin can be when surrounded by the concrete of London.

Some things change, some stay the same. Roller blades have replaced roller skates. A Notting Hill Gate restaurant is no longer a workman's café with tea plus bread and dripping. It's a cosmopolitan affair with Italian or French waiters serving every conceivable nationality on earth. The age of microelectronics has even reached the model yachts on the Round Pond. Four old men sat in deck chairs at the pond's edge with controllers in hand sending radio messages to gadgetry hidden deep in the yachts' hulls, changing the set of sails and the direction of the rudder. However, the topics they chatted to one another about – the weather, the direction of the wind, the obstructions in the pond – were the same as twenty years ago.

Comforting it is too that the Peter Pan still faces the Serpentine with elves at his feet, double-decker buses are red and even the MGB Roadster has the same feel. I sat in a brand-new one in a showroom in the Old Brompton Road. This was a limited edition model powered by a Range Rover engine. The price at £24 500 was different to the £900 I paid for mine in March 1971; but then the interior is more lavish and the engine no doubt packs a greater punch. Thankfully I was informed that the sound – which is why most people buy an MGB anyway – still has that distinctive throaty roar.

Two important events happened whilst I was in England. The Tories suffered a massive drubbing in the local government elections. The Labour leader, Tony Blair, attributed the swing as much to a positive acceptance of New Labour's policies as to disgust over Tory disunity. Blair certainly comes across as a New Age leader but he may find out, as others have before him, that there's many a slip between the cup of policy formulation and the lip of policy implementation. One wonders as well how many socialists of the old guard are waiting in the wings to try and take over the show should he bring the Labour Party to power. Will he have the will to ensure that his more modern vision predominates over theirs? Nevertheless, he has already achieved a great deal in his brief leadership. The last time the Labour Party was so popular was when Harold Wilson was Prime Minister in the 1960s.

The other event was the highlight of the week. It was the celebration of the fiftieth anniversary of VE day, the day World War II ended in Europe in victory for the Allies. Britain is wonderful at pageantry. Royalty came to the fore. The Queen Mother spoke without notes to an enthralled crowd in Hyde Park. Not bad for a 94-year-old. She said: "The day will bring back many memories and I do hope all of you will remember with pride and gratitude those men and women, armed and unarmed, whose courage really brought us to victory. God bless them all." Later Vera Lynn sang "The White Cliffs of Dover", as two grey-haired pensioners resisted an advance from two equally ancient GIs to "come and sit on our knees".

Among war heroes, special attention was given to Airwoman

Daphne Pearson who was awarded the George Cross for helping a pilot get out of his plane which crashed in Kent with undetonated bombs. When one of them subsequently went off, Pearson crouched over the pilot to shield him. In typical British understatement, she recalled it as a "very unique experience".

After the Queen's speech at the Guildhall banquet on Saturday night, an eminent historian was asked on television how young people today should relate to the celebration. He said they should pause to reflect on what their lives would have been like if Hitler had won. Good point. Young girls would probably not have been roller-blading in the sunshine. Restaurants would not have been cosmopolitan. Democracy and royalty would have ceased to exist. The post-war generation have a lot to be thankful for.

A trail of statues

I spent an autumn day in London on the trail of statues. History makes London world class.

29.9.1996 Statues shed light on a nation's history. With that in mind, I set out to inspect some of them in the vicinity of my guest house in South Kensington, London. It was a balmy, autumnal evening in early September, the kind that has a long-lasting twilight.

The first I came upon was at the top of Queen's Gate in front of the entrance to Kensington Gardens. He was an imposing gentleman called Lord Napier of Magdala, Constable of the Tower of London, who lived from 1810 to 1890. It was erected by his countrymen, which is a polite way of saying that they put up the money for it. He must have been a very special constable!

Crossing into the gardens, I noticed some beautiful deer adorning the gates. But the next statue of interest was in the grounds of Kensington Palace facing the Round Pond. It was a young Queen Victoria sculpted in 1837 by her daughter HRH Princess Louise (Victoria was born in Kensington Palace). The statue is delightful because its marble curves reveal a demure young woman in the year of her accession to the throne, before the cares of monarchy had taken their toll.

On the other side of the Round Pond, a classical Greek character bestrides a rearing horse and shields his eyes from the sun. Perfectly representing its name Physical Energy, the statue was the work of G.F. Watts. Further on, hidden in a little grove by the Serpentine, is the famous statue of Peter Pan tooting his pipe while surrounded by rabbits, mice, squirrels and fairies that look suspiciously like Edwardian ladies with wings. J.M. Barrie's famous character was sculpted in bronze by Sir George Frampton in 1912. At the Bayswater end of the Serpentine, among the fountains and the potted plants, sits the physician Jenner (1749-1823) who initiated smallpox vaccination. He looks suitably pensive with manuscript in hand.

In the middle of Hyde Park Corner is the most arresting statue of all: Wellington (1769-1852). He's on horseback with four soldiers, one each from the 1st Guards, 6th Inniskilling Dragoons, 23rd Royal Welsh Fusiliers and 42nd Royal Highlanders, guarding him. With his long sideburns and gnome-like hat, he looks every bit like the "Iron Duke" who defeated Napoleon at the Battle of Waterloo in 1815. In the same area, statues of soldiers in more modern uniforms – three standing and one lying in state – mark the monument commemorating the 49 076 of all ranks of the Royal Regiment of Artillery who gave their lives for King and country in the Great War of 1914-1919 and the 29 924 who were killed in the World War II between 1939 and 1945. The inscription says: "They died with the faith that the future of all mankind would benefit by their sacrifice."

These few statues encapsulate the rise and fall of the little island called Britain. On the one hand, I saw a young queen who was to become the most important person in the world during her reign from 1837 to 1901; the physical energy of the Industrial Revolution; the country's immense reservoir of scientific and literary skills; and the military prowess of a great warrior nation. On the other hand, I sadly reflected on the cost of two World Wars from which Britain has never recovered.

A tale of two cities – Hong Kong and Singapore

Hong Kong and Singapore are contrasting examples of how world-class cities evolve.

16.7.1995 This is a tale of two very different cities – Hong Kong and Singapore. As I flew into Hong Kong the other day on Cathay Pacific, it resembled a mega-Hillbrow by the sea. From the air, the skyscrapers stand upright like giant silvery fishes packed together in neat rows between the shoreline and the dark green heavily forested hills. On closer inspection from ground level, the skyscrapers come in every conceivable shape and size – as though office architects had reserved their most imaginative concepts for Hong Kong.

Interspersed between the skyscrapers in the central district (one of them has the unforgettable name "Sincere Insurance Building") are much shorter, considerably dilapidated, residential tenements. Walking down the main street, one has the feeling that modern Hong Kong has encroached on traditional Chinese Hong Kong in a fairly haphazard way – like kikuyu grass taking over a lawn. The two cultures for the time being sit side by side. On the one hand, there is the late twentieth-century Western culture of hi-tech electronic gizmos, designer labels and all the other artifacts of consumerism. The malls are air-conditioned catacombs of boutiques and department stores bulging with goodies, enough to make even the most acquisitive Sandton City regulars drop before they've finished shopping. Most of the sales girls have cellulars to chat to their friends when they aren't serving customers. On the other hand, take a left or a right turn off the main street and one is immediately in a myriad of narrow alleys full of stalls with meat, fish, vegetables and fruit. The timelessness of the Chinese is exemplified in the lined, aging faces of the stall-holders. As a pedestrian, one never feels the remotest physical threat despite the incredible number of people cramming into the streets at any one time.

The first thing that strikes one about Singapore after arriving from Hong Kong is the greenery. Little room exists for grass, shrubs or trees in the concrete miasma of Hong Kong, although I did see some snails poking their horned heads out from the hotel's herbaceous border after it had rained. But Singapore abounds with parks and grassy verges and flowers and palms. The city's planners have conscientiously balanced the environment with development. The renowned cleanliness and tidiness of the pavements, the orderliness of the traffic flow need to be seen to be believed. The botanical gardens, thank heavens, do not measure up to Kirstenbosch. I walked past the bar which Nick Leeson frequented in his Barings days, overlooking the river. It's a famous tourist attraction now!

The same friend who pointed this feature out to me whilst we were strolling to lunch made an interesting comment: "Sometimes I can't wait to get out of Singapore for a time to experience a little more freedom. However, after I've been away two weeks, I can't wait to get back because I can't stand the chaos on the other side." Therein lies the Confucian-like contradiction of Singapore. People are extremely happy there because of the order in their lives which allows them plenty of personal freedom. Crime is nonexistent. Being found in possession of an unlicensed firearm carries the death penalty.

Yet Hong Kong is also a contradiction. Amidst the chaos of probably the most free-enterprise society in the world, something resembling order prevails. Hong Kong functions pretty well without a grand design. This can be attributed to the self-discipline of the populace. Rule by mainland China looms in 1997, but most Hong-Kongers believe that they will be left alone. Anyway industry is moving northwards because of China's lower wage structure. Integration, in other words, is already taking place.

So, Hong Kong and Singapore represent the yin and the yang of life – the balance of opposites. For out of freedom may come order, but out of order may come freedom. The conundrum will never fade.

Cape Town
Closer to home, Cape Town is very special. One helpful feature in attracting talented young people to a world-class city is the high quality of its educational institutions. Cape Town certainly has that.

18.8.1996 Cape Town sounds like Chicago in the Roaring 20s. The Prohibition era was then in full swing and the king of the "speakeasies" that bootlegged the liquor was Al Capone. Eventually Elliot

113

Ness and his crack squad of policemen who earned the title of "The Untouchables" closed in on him. Capone was convicted of tax evasion in 1931 and put behind bars for eight years. He died of syphilis in 1947.

Headlines in the Mother City convey the same atmosphere. Every day, the placards proclaim a new development in the war against gangsters and drugs – the modern version of a prohibited substance. Hearsay is that these gangs have armouries that would make the Pentagon envious and you can't buy a bullet in Cape Town for love or money. The gun shops are all sold out. The current gangsters don't ride around in upright black limos and they're not dressed in grey fedoras and white spats. But they have the same swagger as Capone and speak as openly to the Press as he did.

Yet, Cape Town is still a place of tranquillity. Last Tuesday in the late afternoon, I went for a walk down Hatfield Street which runs parallel to the Gardens. I wended my way across to Adderley Street. There at 5.30 pm I found a coffee bar still open with a marvellous array of exotically named coffees. Over a cappuccino I eavesdropped on an animated conversation between some young men and women who obviously all worked in the same office. The consensus was that the CEO was only to be seen at press conferences or leading distinguished visitors around the office while exuding an artificial friendliness to the staff.

When I stepped outside again, I noticed the glowering skies over Table Mountain. Inevitably a heavy shower started. While youthful pedestrians danced through the puddles like Gene Kelly, I sought refuge under an awning running alongside some shops. As luck would have it, one of the shops was full of model cars and aeroplanes and the kits out of which they were made. But the object which especially caught my eye through the window was a handsome model yacht with a mast at least three foot high. I thought of all the inland waters in the Western Cape and how fast the yacht would sail in the high winds. What fun it would be to take a few days off to go on a model sailing tour!

After the rain stopped, I walked through the Gardens towards the mountain. Dusk by now had fallen but the squirrels were still busily crossing the thoroughfare. Their grey fur must be waterproof or they must have sheltered from the rain in the hideaways where they store the acorns because they showed no sign of being drenched by the shower. As I turned left out of the gate at the top of the Gardens, I noticed the security guard across the road at the entrance of the Mount Nelson Hotel. He was decked out in one of those uniforms which I used to see on cigarette cards displaying soldiers in their regimental colours. I've kept a few sets from the early 1950s when they were all the rage.

A car approached the entrance. The guard stood stiffly to attention and gave a smart salute. The Mount Nelson will never lose its image of colonial grandeur. It will never cease to attract tourists who look as if they've just disembarked from one of these great liners where aristocratic couples with long cigarette holders charlestoned on the deck in the moonlight. Despite the gangsters, life goes on pretty much as usual.

Parliament Street in Port Elizabeth

Port Elizabeth has a marvellous street as well. The San Francisco coffee bar epitomises the world-class principle of differentiation. It has a chess board!

1.9.1996 It's one of those streets. I came across the following in it: raspberry-flavoured cider vinegar; a Regency brass coal scuttle and shovel with original liner; the narrowest house in South Africa in the "Y" intersection between two streets; a laser eye surgery; a bridal wear shop with the appropriate title of "New Beginnings"; a café with the name "Cyber Joes" which used to be "The Internet Café"; "Kahlua Fudge" and "Columbian Decaf" in another coffee bar called "San Francisco"; and "The Silver Lantern" , "Rattle and Hum" and "The Rusty Nail", names for a Chinese restaurant, a pub and an antique shop respectively.

While strolling along the pavement of this remarkable street, I met the country's top herpetologist (snake and lizard expert) coming the other way. He was accompanied by his wife who assisted George Martin in recording one of the tracks for the Beatles' "Sgt Pepper's Lonely Hearts Club Band" – the definitive album of the 1960s.

Where could all these interesting products and places be? Where can one meet such talented people? The answer is Parliament Street in the

Central suburb of Port Elizabeth. I was down there to address the Eastern Cape Farmers Banquet at the Hotel Edward. Incidentally, on the left inner side of the menu for the banquet, the following phrase appeared after the wines listed: "limited supply available". I guess farmers are renowned for exhausting hotel supplies.

Before the banquet, I had a bit of time to kill so I decided to brave the gusty sea breeze outside. It's not for nothing that PE is called "the windy city". Usually, I stay at Summerstrand, further up the coast. So it was with great pleasure that I came across the Central suburb full of old settlers' houses that have been done up or, to use that horrible London term, "gentrified". Central in fact reminds me of Chelsea with its chic shops and restaurants. But what a wonderful tribute to small business and the diversity of human interest Central is. Only the liberty conferred by the free-market system on entrepreneurs to do their own thing produces a result like this.

Sipping a cup of hot chocolate in the San Francisco with Bill Branch (the herpetologist) and his wife Donvé (the sound engineer) who now makes garden pots for a living, I noticed a couple of men playing chess at another table. Deep in thought as they moved their pieces, they offered an alternative existence to the world of executive stress and deadlines. The woman who owned the café had quit teaching to run a small business. She said it was the best thing she ever did. Mentally, I kept humming: "If you're going to San Francisco, you're sure to meet some gentle people there. All across the nation, there's a strange vibration. People in motion . . . " PE has great appeal. There's comparatively little crime, people stop to smell the roses. Maybe, when I retire one day, I'll put some new strings on the guitar, mosey down to PE from Gauteng and start doing cabaret again.

Ernie

Ernie is truly world class and business can learn a thing or two from him.

22.6.1997 The big man lined up the putt and stroked it with a deft touch. As the ball headed for the hole, he noticed it give a slight wobble as it rolled over a scuff mark on the green left by the spikes of a previous player. It still went into the centre of the cup. After retrieving the ball from the hole, he calmly tapped down the offending protuberance with his putter so that the following pair would not be faced with the same problem.

Was this a Sunday afternoon competition at the local golf club? No, this was America's most prestigious golf tournament – the US Open played last weekend at the Congressional Country Club, Bethesda, Maryland. The big man was none other than our own Ernie Els. He was playing the back nine of the final round. At the time he was in a four-way tie for the lead with Colin Montgomery, his playing partner, and with the final two-ball behind them, Tom Lehman and Jeff Maggart. He didn't have to make it any easier for Tom and Jeff with whom he was competing for the title. But he did and, by so doing, proved that he deserves the accolade "world class". He went on to win the title for the second time as nerves got the better of the other three challengers and he held on at four under par.

The following day another world-class athlete triumphed – Charl Mattheus in the Comrades Marathon. In the final stretch into Durban, he surged ahead of Nic Bester to win by a relatively easy margin. He had taken the trouble to do altitude training in Colorado in preparation for the race. As he said in his interview afterwards, it was money well spent. Indeed, there was something especially sweet about his victory after his unfortunate disqualification in 1992. He had to come back and prove he was the best ultramarathoner in the world. That takes guts and determination of an unusual kind.

The funny thing is that the qualities which make you world class in sport are similar to those that make you world class in business. In sport, focus – keeping your eye on the ball literally and mentally – is everything. The days are gone when you could be a gifted amateur playing a bit of cricket, soccer, rugby, tennis and golf, etc. and expect to be internationally competitive. Denis Compton represented England at cricket and soccer but that was half a century ago. Sport is simply too professional now to do that. Michael Jordan, the American basketball-playing genius, switched to baseball and failed dismally.

Actually, modern sport *is* big business. Branding has therefore become essential for the stars. Arnold Palmer, the legendary golfer, used to have an army following him around the course. The reason was not so much his skill – Jack Nicklaus and Gary Player were his equals – but his aggressive and unique style. He was different. Today we have the Tiger Woods phenomenon. His prodigious length off the tee, plus the way he broke all records and slaughtered the opposition in the Masters at Augusta earlier this year, means that he is already a global icon at 21. But he and Martina Hingis, the teenage tennis prodigy, share one thing in common. They both started playing their respective sports when they were three years old. You have to begin young and have ambitious parents these days.

Yet Ernie exhibited another side of being world class. He's basically a decent guy, a person my son would call a cool dude. Fans remember a generous gesture on the course more than the putts sunk. In business, it's the same. A healthy bottom line is a result that shareholders expect. However, when business does something which is motivated by plain old virtue as opposed to profit, the action is unexpected and far more memorable in the eyes of the general public.

When the broad-shouldered champ gave his parents a bear hug after walking off the eighteenth green, I thought to myself "you're worth waiting up for. You've got what it takes. The private sector can learn a thing or two from you. Yes, you really are something else." Chuckling at the unintended pun, I switched off the television and went to bed.

Tiger

I feel chuffed that I spotted Tiger when he was still an amateur. He stood out for the same reason as Ernie.

24.9.1995   It was like the opening sequence of the film *Chariots of Fire*. Remember the British squad running along the beach in final preparation for the Olympics? As they splashed through the shallow waves, their faces exuded the sheer delight of athletes at their prime.

The actual scene to which I'm referring took place a fortnight ago at Royal Porthcawl, a golf course on the coast of Wales. The event was the Walker Cup which is contested between the best amateur golfers from America on the one hand and Great Britain and Ireland on the other. Gordon Sherry, a huge Scot and the mainstay of the latter side, was pitted against Chris Riley in the first singles match on the final Sunday afternoon. In heavy and continuous rain, Sherry struck a nine iron to within four feet of the par-four eighteenth hole to give him victory over the American. To see this giant, his hair awry and his clothes sodden, punch the air with his fist and pirouette around the green in celebration gave one the same sense of exhilaration as watching *Chariots of Fire*. Englishman David Howell, Scot Stephen Gallacher and the Irish undertaker Jody Fanagan followed Sherry in with victories.

This put the result beyond doubt and the Great Britain and Ireland side took the cup for only the fourth time in 34 contests since 1922. Clive Brown, the nonplaying Welsh captain, said: "It was a dream to be here in the first place but to win the Walker Cup here in Wales is something I never thought would happen to me, or in my lifetime."

However, what really made this tournament stand out for me was something that happened on the previous day at the eighteenth hole. It was late afternoon and the sun was setting behind the green, making it difficult to judge distance to the hole. The wind was gusting and the players in the final singles match – Gary Wolstenholme and Tiger Woods – had tricky second shots to play. The English Wolstenholme hit a fairly indifferent but safe shot close to the green. Woods, an American teenage golfing prodigy, hooked his ball badly and ended up in a ditch well to the left of the green. This shot cost him the match as the ball was ruled to be out of bounds.

The manner in which this young man accepted his misfortune

made him a true champion in my eyes. He calmly confirmed the situation with the referee and picked up the ball. At the conclusion of the match he shook his opponent's hand warmly. He generally handled his emotions with the utmost dignity. It was so different to the histrionics that we have become accustomed to see from professionals in many sports when they feel fate or the referee has been cruel to them. They rant and rave. They argue. They give a bad example to the young.

Maybe I'm old-fashioned. But to witness players giving their all for no money and behaving impeccably as well makes one feel very good. There is something special about amateur sport. It has a refreshing innocence about it. And, by the way, Woods beat the same opponent convincingly the following day. He's made of the right stuff.

World rugby champions
If we can be world class at rugby, why not in our economy as well? I still get a tingle from the memory.

2.7.1995 The Boks did it. World champions. Against the odds. There will never be a moment like it again. Even if they win in Wales in 1999, you can never beat the first time. The sheer freshness of it. In front of their own crowd. It's like Halley's Comet. You are very lucky to witness it once in a lifetime – twice is almost a miracle.

The best comment in the aftermath came in an advert: "Together we achieved a far greater victory than the winning of the cup. We earned the right to play for it." Yes, it was more than a rugby match. In that sense, a win for South Africa was more significant for South Africa than a win by the All Blacks for New Zealand. Perhaps a bit of divine intervention accompanied our team?

Everyone will carry away different memories from the day. I was fortunate enough to be at Ellis Park to see our President in his Springbok kit greeting the teams while the crowd chanted "Nelson, Nelson, Nelson". The new South African flag really is attractive when waved by thousands of people at the same time. I can't see it being a temporary phenomenon. The fellow who designed it has probably left his mark for many generations to come.

The game itself was edge-of-the-seat stuff because of the closeness of the score. The absence of tries did not detract from the spectacle. It was incredible how quickly the play moved from one end to the other because of the accuracy of the kicking. From the stands, Jonah Lomu did not quite look the giant he does on television though his thighs are awesomely large. Whenever he was tackled the crowd were delirious. What it is to be a marked man. Yet the game was clean, which shows the deterrent value of summary justice.

With the scores tied just before the end of the game, the announcement over the loudspeaker was ominous: a tie would mean extra time and a tie after extra time would mean a win for the team with the most tries and if the tries (or lack of them) were even then the team with the least number of players sent off during the tournament would win. That information conveyed one message – that the Boks had to win or they would lose. The gloom over the penalty for the All Blacks just into extra time was only lifted with the penalty later awarded to the Boks. And then the drop goal. Stransky will replay that one on his VCR for the rest of his life. And so will we.

But the best bit was when the game was over. The cup looked like solid gold. It had that deep yellowish tinge of 24 carats. It would, however, have been too heavy to hoist above the head. What the hell, as the Boks made their way around the pitch, they could have carried anything. Three sporting gestures were noteworthy: the way the small New Zealand contingent clapped the Boks as they passed their corner of the stands; Francois Pienaar hurrying across the field to shake the hands of the few All Black players who had come out to thank their supporters (including Lomu); and Pienaar's speech which was all grace and no boast.

The car ride home was exciting. The residents of the small homes just outside the grounds were all on their porches waving to the cars. Everybody was honking their horns and at most traffic lights up Jan Smuts Avenue students danced among the motorists. Flags were everywhere, patriotism was rife and the euphoria was rainbow-like. We even persuaded one police car to celebrate by turning on its flashing blue lights.

I took my son to the game. He plays flank in his under-15 school team. I thought back to the great sporting events I had watched in my

121

youth: Jim Laker taking nineteen wickets for England in a cricket test against the Australians and England winning the soccer world cup with Geoff Hurst scoring brilliantly. June 24, however, has to take pride of place. My son will duly recount the splendour of the day and name the heroes one by one to his kids. He was particularly impressed by how low the 747 swooped over the stadium before the game started! For me, the result bore out two hackneyed expressions: no guts, no glory; no pain, no gain. If only the country as a whole took these lessons to heart, we could be the first African dragon.

Gogga
Gogga is a great thing to happen to South African cricket. He's a world-class "leggie".

7.1.1996 Gaga over Gogga. Translated into plain English, a little bit crazy over Paul Adams. But why shouldn't we be? It is not every day that a country produces a leg-spinning sensation who has the potential to be a match winner at Test level.

As I studied him on television, the aspect I liked is that he really "tweaks" the ball. His unorthodox action, together with plenty of wrist at the moment of delivery, combine to make the ball spin like a top during flight. That means he can turn the ball appreciably – just like Shane Warne – on even the flattest of wickets. There are so many spinners around in county cricket in England and provincial cricket here who actually are no more than slow seamers. They don't get the kick when the ball hits the ground. Sure, they conscientiously bowl a good length, they are consistent and they keep the run rate down. But they lack the magic because a batsman has to make a mistake for them to claim his wicket.

By contrast, Adams and Warne have the ability to bowl out a batsman even when he is playing a good shot. They can bowl a right-hander out around his legs, have him caught at slip with a ball that moves away at an unplayable angle or get him trapped lbw with a camouflaged delivery that breaks back into him. It is beautiful to watch the discomfort of a top-class batsman at the mercy of a genuine spin artist. There is no element of intimidation with bouncers or beating the bat with sheer pace. The contest is purely a mental one – the batsman's concentration against the spinner's guile.

I bowled leg spinners for a time. I was taught to do so at the Sandham, Strudwick and Gover indoor cricket school at Wandsworth in London. The coaches there adopted me because I was the youngest client of the cricket school at seven years old. My mother used to take me every Thursday of the school holidays on a No. 28 bus from Kensington. After the session in the nets, we would have tea in the small canteen adjoining the playing area. Many famous cricketers of the time would join us for a friendly chat. Arthur Wellard was my favourite coach. He used to play for Somerset, had huge hands and was a legend for hitting the ball prodigious distances.

So I know how difficult it is to keep line and length as a leg spinner, especially when somebody is slogging you all over the field. That's why Adams looks such a good bowler. He doesn't seem disconcerted when a batsman is taking runs off him. Indeed, he says: "I'm not discouraged when I'm hit for a four or a six. It's only when I know I've bowled a bad ball, then I'm angry, but at myself."

Good for him. In my case, I switched to fast bowling later in my school career as I was frustrated by the delicacy of touch required of a "leggie". At six foot four, I was able to get the lift off the pitch. Even though I was quite erratic, I managed to take nine wickets for one run during a one-day school match. We still lost the match. Is that a record?

Finally, a few words of advice for young Paul. Don't let your head be turned by the fame and the fans. Glamour is very superficial. Remember that your family, your friends and your team-mates will be watching you closely to see how you handle your good fortune. Be a role model for all the other kids who play cricket, soccer or rugby on the streets and dream of being an overnight success like you. Above all, enjoy your immediate future because the process of getting to the top is the happiest experience you'll have. Once you are there, the strength of character needed to stay at the top is the sign of true greatness. But the thrill is never quite the same.

Bafana Bafana

Bafana Bafana were magnificent in winning the African Nations soccer cup. Another lesson for creating a rainbow economy.

11.2.1996   African pride. It was apparent everywhere in the crowd who watched Bafana Bafana beat Tunisia in the final of the African Nations soccer cup last Saturday. It was captured in that wonderful photograph of Neil Tovey, flanked by Nelson Mandela, holding the cup aloft after the game. I've never seen our president looking so jubilant as he punched both fists into the air. As a nation, we rejoiced with him.

An article written the day before the soccer final by Thami Mazwai in *Business Day* had the prophetic headline "Time has come to be African". He is editor of *Enterprise*, a business journal. Mazwai was describing popular reaction to an interview he had on television with Tim Modise three weeks previously. The discussion focused on what being African entailed. In Mazwai's own words, "being African has nothing to do with colour, but everything to do with being of the continent of Africa, body and soul. The black reaction to the Modise interview shocked even me. A torrent of pride gushed out. What I said touched a raw nerve. Indeed, the indigenous people are still denied the right of being themselves, and foreign customs and ways of life hold sway. The new SA is becoming an extension of Europe or the US. Our country desperately needs an infusion of itself and, to balance the equation, some form of exorcism. We cannot bottle ourselves up any longer."

These strong sentiments are no doubt making a section of the white community shudder. Unfortunately, I can offer no solace to them. As another weekly columnist has bluntly observed, the whites who go with the flow in regard to Mazwai's theme will retain considerable influence in this country's affairs. Those who don't won't. Bob Dylan put it a little more poetically: "You better start swimming or you'll sink like a stone, for the times they are a-changin'."

Yet the example of soccer brings hope, because it identifies the true objective towards which we should all be striving. Pride with no prejudice. Every member of Bafana Bafana earned his place on sheer merit. Some players such as Mark Fish, who may be joining Manchester United, are obviously world class. Clive Barker, the coach, did not have to perform some intricate juggling act to arrive at the politically correct ratio in respect of the team's colour. The rainbow was genuine. No one was prejudiced. The result was victory.

Would that we had a similar state of affairs in business! But we're a long way from rainbow ownership and rainbow management (plus of course we're talking male and female in business too). So how do we get the corporate world from here to where soccer is today and at the same time ensure that like our national soccer team we win against the competition?

Clive Barker points the way when he echoes Mazwai's plea for a change of attitude: "I keep saying to the players: 'If we play like Germany we'll never beat Germany; if we play like the Dutch we'll never beat them either. But if we play like South Africa there are no limits'." That's it. Let's give every kid here a shot at becoming an entrepreneur by providing the requisite skills as well as access to capital. Let's make it as easy as kicking a ball in the streets. Moreover, let's instil in that young person the same passion for business that exists for soccer and say "do it the South African way". Then maybe, sometime in the foreseeable future, we shall look back with pride at how the younger generation achieved a rainbow economy that is the envy of the world.

Marathon gold
Josia came from nowhere to win Olympic gold.

11.8.1996   I was out of my chair, jumping up and down, urging on the diminutive figure running on TV. Then Josia Thugwane made his last surge as the three leaders of the Marathon wound their way through the skyscrapers in downtown Atlanta towards the finish at the Olympic stadium. I couldn't believe that the commentators didn't say something the instant he moved ahead. They left it for a few seconds! And then there was a nail-biting five-minute period as I expected either the Korean or the Kenyan to respond and narrow the gap again. But our man, his face impassive behind shades and as cool as a cucumber, maintained his lead. When he entered the stadium, I knew he had won. So I sat back and luxuriated in the last minute of the race while the crowd cheered him on around the track. And just prior to breasting the tape, he made a small gesticulation of joy – pointing a finger to the sky to illustrate he was number one.

For me, it had to be the most magic sporting event since Jim Laker, the offspinner, took nineteen wickets for England when playing Australia at Old Trafford in 1956. I watched that Test on a black-and-white TV at the age of eleven. I guess it was fitting that Josia performed his feat almost forty years to the day after Jim. What a story the papers had to tell! A courageous underdog, an unknown coal miner, a rank amateur came to Atlanta, took on the best in the world and won. Like Julius Caesar: he came, he saw, he conquered. He was as terse about his victory as well: "I didn't give myself a chance before the race, but once we were into it I felt good. There have been a lot of sacrifices but it's all been worth it."

What is the origin of the Marathon race? You have to go back to 490 BC. In that year, King Darius of Persia prepared a vast army and built a great fleet to carry his soldiers across the Aegean Sea to attack Athens. He mustered 100 000 men, all well armed and strong. The Persian galleys entered Marathon Bay to the northeast of Athens. When the Athenians heard of the landing, they summoned 9 000 men and started for Marathon at once. But, outnumbered more than ten to one, they were in despair. Miltiades, the general in command, said that there was only one way to attack the Persians. They had to run at full tilt down the hill and startle the enemy. And so it was to be. The enemy were amazed by the bravery of the Athenians. The two wings of the mighty Persian army were forced back to the sea. Only the centre held. So the Athenians re-formed themselves into a tightly knit wedge and attacked the centre. After fierce fighting, the Persian's line was broken altogether and the soldiers fled hastily to their ships.

Miltiades called for Pheidippides, a well-known athlete, to run at full speed to Athens to spread the good news of victory. The distance from Marathon to Athens by road was measured at 26 miles and 385 yards (just over 42 km) and now represents the length of the modern race. It is not known how long it took Pheidippides to get to Athens with his spectacular announcement, but we do gather from the records that he dropped dead with exhaustion after he had conveyed the news.

Tough little Josia completed the Marathon in 2 hours, 12 minutes and 36 seconds and he didn't drop dead. Instead, he performed a marvellous victory lap around the stadium wrapped in the South African flag. With that, he wrote his name into the history books and earned a place in all our hearts. Rightly so. His win was as outstanding as the Greek one at Marathon 2 586 years ago.

Viva Amakrokokroko
Viva Amakrokokroko. You inspire us.

8.9.1996 *The Star* had them on the front page in green-and-gold tracksuit tops wearing their medals. For the record, the team claimed 28 medals – ten golds, eight silvers and ten bronzes. They established two new world records – for wheelchair javelin and men's 50-metre freestyle in swimming. Tokyo Sexwale welcomed them home last weekend wearing a T-shirt proclaiming "Viva Amakrokokroko". He said: "We can all learn from what they have achieved. Even if you come disabled, your spirit can continue."

He was talking about South Africa's 41-member team who participated in the "paralympics" that took place in Atlanta directly after the Olympic Games. What a great achievement that we finished fifteenth in the overall national rankings. National Paralympic Committee of SA president Peter Goldhawk set his sights even higher: "We eventually want a team that will win the Games."

This indomitable attitude is shared by the man who appeared on the front cover of *Time* two weeks ago – Christopher Reeve. Paralysed from the neck down by a riding accident during a competition in May last year, he still has laser-blue eyes and the Superman look. *Time* cleverly called him "Super Man" on the cover because of what he has done to raise money since his accident for spinal-cord-injury research. In September last year, he appeared on television with Barbara Walters and said that on his fiftieth birthday he would like to stand and raise a glass to all who helped him. He is now 43. He adds in the article: "When John Kennedy promised that by the end of the 1960s we would put a man on the moon, everybody – including the scientists – shook their heads in dismay. But we did it. We can cure spinal-cord injuries too, if there's a will. What was possible in outer space is possible in inner space."

That may not be an impossible dream when one reads about the ground-breaking research being done at Sweden's Karolinska Institute in Stockholm. The scientists there took adult rats whose spinal cords were completely severed and transplanted nerves from elsewhere in the body to bridge the gap. Lars Olsen and his colleagues managed to get the nerves at the injury site to regenerate and produce "functional recovery". Dr Wise Young of New York University put it in layman's terms: "The rats walked!"

The journal *Science* is quick to point out that the Stockholm technique will not be of immediate use to humans because very few spinal-cord injuries result in totally severed cords. Yet the bridging technique is proof of concept, namely something that had been regarded as impossible is possible. Reeve exclaimed on hearing the Stockholm news: "If that's what they're doing over there, bring me to them. I'm a rat!"

So there's hope. Meanwhile, let's raise a glass to our paralympic team. You did magnificently. Here's looking at you, kids!

Chelsea's victory
Finally Chelsea prove that they are world class.

25.5.1997 The magic moment I've been waiting for all my life came sooner than expected. I was just sitting down in front of a television set in Pretoria on Saturday a week ago when the Italian picked the ball up in his own half. He didn't do a convoluted continental dribble or flick a short pass. In the brilliant May sunshine, he set off like a racehorse down the home stretch at Ascot and beat the defenders through sheer speed. Seeing the goalkeeper off his line, he let fly with the big dipper. The ball sped over the goalie's outstretched hands to clip the underside of the bar and land in the net. Chelsea had scored against Middlesbrough in soccer's premier FA Cup Final at Wembley.

Roberto Di Matteo achieved what Bob Chatt had done for Aston Villa against West Bromwich in the year when Marconi sent a message over a mile by wireless, Röntgen discovered X-rays and Jameson mounted his famous raid on the third last day of December. Chatt scored a goal after about forty seconds of the match in 1895; Di

Matteo repeated the feat 102 years later if you add a couple of seconds. Chelsea went on to score one more goal in the second half to seal victory. But I knew my side had won as soon as the Italian slotted that wondrous opening goal.

I have supported Chelsea ever since I parted company with my nappies and became conscious of the external world in the late 1940s. Being brought up in Church Street in Kensington, I was just a bus ride costing a few pence away from Stanford Bridge, Chelsea's home ground. Many a cold winter's Saturday afternoon I would stand in "The Shed" where all the hard-core Chelsea fans would gather. With our frosted breath and blue rosettes, we would cheer the team on with a variety of war cries. These were usually based on contemporary pop melodies with amended lyrics. In the "bovver boy" era of the 1960s, fights would frequently erupt in the stands. In fact, it got so bad that the police confiscated the bovvers' belts and braces as they entered the turnstiles so they had to hold up their trousers during the match. That way they couldn't indulge in fisticuffs. The said items of apparel were duly returned on departure from the stadium. I had my nice warm duffel coat and scarf to protect me against the elements. Thankfully, the police never interfered with me!

Names like Jimmy Greaves with a finesse almost equal to Georgie Best, Peter Osgood the aggressive centre forward, and the ebullient Tommy Docherty – "The Doc" as he was called during his tenure of manager – come to mind in my era at "The Shed". Of course, it's nothing like that now. As the commentator remarked, Chelsea resembles the United Nations, with players from France, Denmark, Italy and Romania in the team. We have Mexican waves in the stands.

Chelsea's manager, Ruud Gullit, is a Dutch superstar. It's his first year at the Bridge and he accomplished what no other foreign manager has ever done – to lead an English club to victory in the FA cup. I have a feeling his dreadlocks are going to be a customary sight for Chelsea fans for a few seasons or more. As he said later: "I am very emotional. My team were thoroughly professional. The atmosphere was fantastic. It was perfect!"

Amen. And for me it was wonderful to see Denis Wise, the captain who looks a bit like a bovver boy himself, raise the cup as he received it from the Duchess of Kent – a broad grin on his cheeky face. As for

Mark Hughes, he has always been one of my favourite forwards even when he played for Manchester United. But I prefer him in blue. Indeed, I'll forgive him for playing for so long for the wrong team now that he is the inspiration behind Chelsea's attack. Well done to him too for going into the record book with four cup winner's medals out of five finals. Yo!

St Mark's and UCT

St Mark's and UCT are both world class but then they have Peter and Mamphela as leaders.

7.9.1997 If you drive to Bronkhorstspruit east of Pretoria and then head northeast through Groblersdal, you eventually land up in Jane Furse, a scattered settlement in the middle of Sekhukhuneland. The harsh and dry environment demands much but gives little. However, the impoverished community is blessed with a world-class private school called St Mark's College. The College opened in 1985 in the derelict buildings of an old mission station. It has however raised sufficient funds to build proper classrooms and dormitories and now caters for 400 students. But the heart of the school's academic life is its library, possessing books ranging from the simplest readers to those written by the greatest minds of the ages. Another gem is the computer centre which is lovingly looked after by an American academic on a year's sabbatical in South Africa.

Peter Anderson, the headmaster, says: "We are building a school that will last for hundreds of years because it is based on principles that will stand the test of time. We believe in the creation of inspired lives through the miracle of hard work." St Mark's regularly achieves a 100 per cent matric pass rate and plenty of university entrances in an area where educational standards have been appallingly low.

At the other end of South Africa is the University of Cape Town. It has taken on a new lease of life with Mamphela Ramphele as its vice chancellor. This demanding lady has the academic and administrative staff really fired up because of her determination to ensure that UCT maintains its world-class reputation. Thus, the common thread running through St Mark's and UCT is highly competent and motivated people who believe in delivering high-quality education to the students. If outcomes-based education is to be successful, it needs people of such calibre to put it into practice.

Focus has always played a prominent role in education. World-class schools have particular characters. In Britain, Winchester is famous for its scholars and classical education, Gordonstoun for its emphasis on outward-bound activities. You don't mess around with a traditional brand name that's taken several centuries to build up. It is unthinkable that Oxford and Cambridge will ever be knocked off their perch as Britain's most famous seats of learning. But, to the discerning student, Oxford is a university more attuned to the arts and humanities while Cambridge inclines to science and mathematics. Microsoft recently announced that it would invest $80 million in establishing a research laboratory at Cambridge. Other than having talented researchers and students, the reason behind the choice is that Cambridge is the hub for more than 300 technology firms in eastern England.

You can picture a world-class educational establishment as a house with a few tall chimneys. There is an irreducible core of academic and sporting activities which an institution requires to be called a school or university. Parents still look to the latter to turn their child into a well-rounded individual. That's the house. But thereafter you need a few specialities which stick out like chimneys on the skyline to make you instantly recognisable. In South Africa, rugby is the hallmark of Maritzburg College. By contrast, the nurturing of sensitive pupils distinguishes Redhill School in Johannesburg and the capacity to produce budding journalists Rhodes University in Grahamstown. These are niches they've made their own.

At the tertiary level in South Africa, a shake-out is inevitable as state subsidies are cut. The market is simply not big enough to afford duplication any more. Universities and technikons will seek greater focus by shedding noncore studies and concentrating on their stronger courses. Each will develop into a particular centre of excellence. One such could be a centre of African studies. After all, what better place to study the history of this continent than at a university located on it. Students from all over the globe could be attracted here if a really comprehensive programme was set up.

Two other world-class attributes are relevant in the educational field. The first is innovation – particularly in the provision of distance education and outreach programmes for disadvantaged communities.

Distance learning also offers a great opportunity for tertiary institutions to specialise and reach a wider audience, possibly overseas as well. Moreover, closer research links between industry and commerce need to be explored. The second attribute relates to instilling a sense of social and environmental responsibility into pupils. This goes without saying in the modern world.

School league tables
Friendly rivalry makes schools better in the UK.

27.11.1994 According to last weekend's London *Sunday Times*, Rhyn Park School in St Martin's Village, Shropshire, is very special indeed. In the national league table of GCSE results, it has climbed 3 000 places in little over four years. It is Britain's most improved school.

The headmistress, Janet Warwick, has transformed the school from just another comprehensive going nowhere in a struggling pit village to one where pupils give of their best not only in class, but also in music, the arts and sport. Each department of the school is held fully accountable for its results. The work ethic is awesome, Janet Warwick herself often putting in more than eighty hours a week. It is no longer "cool" for children to disrupt class or get through school with minimum effort.

This success story would not have come to light in Britain's national press but for the existence of a league table of academic results. It is a pity that in South Africa such a table is so bitterly opposed by many members of the teaching fraternity. The arguments against publishing one are varied.

The most common argument is that the table would concentrate on only one dimension of schooling, namely academic excellence. Ranking schools on this sole criterion would ignore all the other facets of education which contribute towards turning out a well-rounded person. There are two answers to this. One has to do with what the *Daily Telegraph* currently does every year: it gets its education correspondents to provide brief commentaries on as many schools as possible so that the public have a broader picture of the options available.

The second point is that parents are not so dumb as to select a school

133

solely on academic grounds. It will be one of many considerations including proximity to home, level of fees, emphasis on sport, choirs and bands, courses on entrepreneurial skills, mountaineering and other outward-bound activities, more specialised pastimes like collecting butterflies and chess, the gentleness or discipline of the principal, the proportion of boarding to day scholars, the historical tradition, whether or not a parent went to the school, etc., etc. Most important of all is the perception of whether one's offspring will fit in or not. It is therefore highly unlikely that the publishing of a league table will do more than exert some influence over the final outcome of which school a boy or girl goes to.

Another oft-cited complaint about academic ranking is that it will be unfavourably biased towards rich schools. For they can be choosy about intake, they have the lowest pupil-to-teacher ratios and they are able to offer a much wider range of facilities than their poorer counterparts. Drawing attention to this fact in a league table will mean that rich schools will get more applicants and the poor schools less, so the divergence will increase even more. However, the example I quoted at the beginning of this article would suggest that children from any background in any area will perform better than average provided the school has dedicated staff. I know that the resources available to each school in this country vary considerably more than in Britain. To counter this, improvement in ranking should be as newsworthy as – if not more so than – absolute ranking.

A further objection in the past has been the perceived differences in examination standards between the provinces and between the state and the private schools. A combined league table is therefore regarded as a useless apples-and-pears exercise. This argument, though, can be turned on its head by saying that if such differences exist, then a table will expose them as people argue to and fro over the fairness of the results. This should raise standards all around.

The undoubted upside of a league table is that it will invoke a direct comparison between schools, which at the moment is confined to the sports field. It certainly will give parents an important yardstick on which to judge the merits of individual schools. It will enhance some reputations and diminish others. It will be surprising and interesting. For example, of the top thirty schools in Britain's GCSE results, twenty last year were girls-only schools. In this country, if a newspaper ever screwed up the courage to publish a national matriculation list, I would lay a bet that the two top schools would be girls-only schools: Durban Girls' College in Natal and Roedean in the Transvaal. One wonders where all the other illustrious names would feature on the list!

Voluntary retrenchments

Please don't allow this to happen again.

21.7.1996   Given that education is the No. 1 characteristic of a "winning nation" because we're competing in a knowledge-intensive world; and given that South Africa has a critical shortage of skilled teachers, it's hard at first to believe the headline "Thousands of teachers apply for retrenchment". But it's for real – around 5 000 teachers in Gauteng and 2 300 in the Western Cape have applied. For two associated reasons. Firstly, in order to equalise the teacher-to-pupil ratio across all provinces, schools in provinces with higher ratios are being forced to shed staff. Secondly, because the government has committed itself to a policy of keeping compulsory retrenchment to a minimum, staff who don't want to run the risk of being redeployed to other provinces can volunteer for severance packages linked to their accumulated pension benefits. However, those taking packages forfeit the chance of being re-employed by state schools elsewhere.

Theoretically, this sounds like a sensible and humane way of meeting the noble end of equality of opportunity for South African children. However, one has to question whether the dimunition of educational resources in one province will in practice lead to the upliftment of the quality of education in another province. Or will we just equalise down? Teachers are a pretty immobile group because the majority of them are female and many of them are married. The latter are unlikely to move with their kids settled at schools and their husbands in jobs. Moreover, teachers who have the requisite skills, particularly in science and mathematics, that enable them to move to the private sector will probably take the package and do so rather than relocate to a school in an alien neighbourhood.

What about money, though? Well, yes, there are savings in the budgets of the provinces that have down-sized which can be transferred to the provinces short-changed in the past. Nevertheless, I would dispute that the poor state of education in disadvantaged areas is solely due to a shortage of funds. I was taken around a township school the other day by the local shebeen owner. The buildings, although only twelve years old, were in a bad state of disrepair. Only two classrooms were functional and only one toilet operational in two toilet blocks. The school served as a primary school in the morning and a secondary school in the afternoon. The shebeen owner informed me of the heroic efforts of three female teachers from the local community who worked incredible hours to cover the two shifts of the pupils.

There was evidence of the quality of their teaching in the mathematical equations chalked up on one of the blackboards in use. In contrast, the shebeen owner told me that the community had lost faith in the two headmasters who had been imposed from outside. They showed no interest in the kids, they neglected maintenance of the property and they treated every weekend as a long weekend. He couldn't wait to see the back of both of them.

But now for the kicker. He went on to say that a surveyor had pitched up out of the blue at the school site to announce that the provincial authorities had decided to erect another eight classrooms on the property and they'd already awarded the contract to an out-of-town builder. What madness! So the possible salary to be saved of the only male head of department at a primary school in the Western Cape who looks after all the sport there and who will probably have to leave because he was the last HOD to be appointed will be consumed on building unwanted classrooms in another part of the country. What should happen is for the two headmasters to be sacked and the three female teachers to be given large bonuses and promoted.

On a more positive note, arguably the best state secondary school in the country has already planned for the change. The headmaster told me that he has to reduce his staff from 39 to 29, given that the complement of his school lies between 750 and 800. He plans to raise his fees from R3 000 to R4 200 a year and pay six extra teachers out of the increased fees (via the Department of course). This still compares favourably with annual fees of R18 000 for private schools. The elite state schools will survive!

Saxonwold Primary
Saxonwold Primary always lifts my heart when I walk by. What a brilliant example of integration.

25.8.1996 It has been a bad fortnight for South Africa. We have had the row over the revelations by Holomisa, the row over rugby administration, the murder of a senior employee of a foreign company when his car was hijacked in Gauteng, a multiplicity of other violent crimes and the plummeting of the rand to new lows.

It is enough to depress even the most seasoned optimist. So, I do what I always do when I need to shake off the blues. I go for an early morning walk past the Saxonwold Primary School in Johannesburg. Usually when I pass, young mothers are dropping off their children, all smartly turned out in their blue uniforms. One has to run the gauntlet of two groups of young traffic wardens who stop everything in sight (including me as a pedestrian) in order to let one of their own cross the road. With bright orange hats, whistles and a drill which rivals that of the most disciplined army battalion, they zealously perform their duties. Power goes even to the youngest head!

Before the school bell goes, the grounds are teeming with little groups of kids at play. What lifts my heart is that the scene is totally integrated. Boys and girls, who are black, white, Indian and coloured mix it up with one another in a totally unselfconscious way. They are really enjoying each other's company. The outcome of their games is far more important to them than the politics and the crime that we adults worry ourselves sick about. The school has all the magic of the world of Peter Pan and Christopher Robin. Of course, the scene is no different in any other happy and successful junior school anywhere in the world. Nevertheless, it is the truest expression of the New South Africa, the one that I dreamed about in the apartheid years.

Unfortunately, the situation is not repeated in such a spontaneous way for older age groups. At the most conscientious of secondary schools, a certain amount of polarisation along colour lines takes place. Likewise, tertiary institutions, such as universities and technikons, have the same experience. It seems that from teenagerhood on, black and white consciousness creeps in. The old saying of birds of a feather flocking together begins to apply, albeit in a voluntary manner now – it is no longer decreed by law.

As for adult South Africa, progress towards a rainbow nation is very slow in the place where it counts – the lives of ordinary people. We must admit it: we have precious little social integration as yet to match the political transformation. It is seldom that one sees mixed couples walk into a restaurant, and dinner parties tend still to be of one hue. It is a shame, but those advertisements on TV showing jolly camaraderie between the races are not yet reality. The majority of whites here probably have never visited a township home. Work is the only place that the races really come together. After hours they generally go their separate ways.

So, it is up to the next generation to create a properly integrated society. Not because they have to, but because they want to. Let South Africa succeed and be an example for America to follow. Meanwhile, I shall continue to walk by Saxonwold Primary and delight in the ray of sunshine it offers me and must offer all the teachers and parents associated with the school. As we go through these dark times, one must hold the good things about South Africa as closely as one can. That way, the dream will live on.

Parents' gift
The best thing my parents ever gave me was a world-class education.

25.12.1994 Christmas inevitably brings back memories of childhood. If one is lucky enough to have been brought up in a loving family of reasonable means, the memories include fragile Christmas tree decorations and spectacular toys. The latter need not have been expensive, but they were usually unbreakable and repeatedly fun to play with.

I was given four such toys. The first was a Bassett Lowke "O" gauge steam engine. Every other little boy had a Hornby electric train – I had a genuine steam engine. The trouble was that despite having a speed regulator which one gingerly turned to allow steam into the pistons, the engine essentially had two states: stationary and flat out. It would annoyingly derail from the tracks which I had carefully laid out in the sitting room. The methylated spirit wicks under the boiler would then set the carpet alight. This would have to be put out before play was resumed.

The second and third toys were used in tandem – a bicycle and a small model yacht. The former I used to get me from the flat we lived in just off Kensington Church Street in central London to the Round Pond in Kensington Gardens; and the latter I launched from one end of the pond to the other, learning in the process how to set the sails to tack against the wind or run before it. I even had a pole to stop the keel scratching against the rim of the pond as the boat arrived. There were many words of advice from the older "professionals" who frequented the Round Pond with their beautiful six-foot tall craft. These had impossibly complicated steering mechanisms to adjust automatically to every shift in the wind.

The fourth present was a ukulele. Transfer of ownership did not take place under the Christmas tree. Instead, on Christmas Eve my mother and I were doing last-minute shopping in the Portobello Market not far from where we lived. By chance, we came across a second-hand shop with a ukulele in the window. It was a spontaneous decision, proposed by me and seconded by my mother, to buy this musical instrument. I never approached the technical skill of George Formby, but I learnt fairly quickly to play two songs proficiently: "Davy Crockett" and "Clementine". My nickname "Clem" dates from the moment my friends clicked that Clementine and I shared a common feature – an abnormal shoe size. My real Christian name is Christopher.

The ukulele led to a Spanish guitar two years later from my Australian sheep-rearing godfather, whose rare visits to England I eagerly awaited because he could be relied on for decent presents. The new instrument was put to instant commercial use, as I graduated to playing "skiffle" and folk in a Soho coffee bar with a school friend. I did most of the singing, he played a mean guitar. His voice in fact was so flat that his solo vocal efforts were always drowned out by the coffee lady coincidentally deciding to froth the milk when he opened his mouth.

The greatest gift my parents bestowed on me had nothing to do with Christmas. They gave me the best education on offer in England – Winchester College and Oxford University. It gave me an open ticket to work anywhere I liked. It led me to South Africa which I have never regretted. Perhaps we should all make a solemn pledge on December 25th. We will make some tangible contribution in the New Year to give some kids somewhere in South Africa a better chance at getting a decent education. Merry Christmas!

School days

School days go so fast, especially for parents. My son went to The Ridge and St John's College, both of which are world class. So I passed on to my son what my parents gave me.

22.10.1995 Last Sunday, my son announced to me that he was about to spend his last week at school before proceeding on matric study leave. This fact, he asserted, had made him apprehensive about the future because he had imagined that his relatively care-free school days would never end. Term-time basically comprised weekend mountain-biking with his mates interspersed with the more serious pursuit of learning from Monday to Friday. In other words, he was one of those fortunate pupils who later on recall school as "the best days of our lives".

If the idea of a forthcoming major discontinuity was uncomfortable for him, it came as a considerable shock to me. It seemed like only yesterday that I photographed him on the front lawn at home before he set out for his first day at school. His school days for me went by in a flash – much, much shorter than my own. Now it is obvious that our own childhood memories are more comprehensive than the memories we have of our children's childhood. After all, as parents, we are living our own lives, the children are living theirs and occasionally the two intersect for a brief hello/goodbye in the morning, a meal in the evening, shared pastimes at the weekend (my son alas can now outdrive me at golf) and holidays at the beach/mountains/game reserve. We experience our kids in episodes.

But isn't it a pity that at the time we can really enjoy the company of our own children we are usually at the most absorbing part of our careers? When they're gone – to university, to a job in another town, to a spouse – it is then that we have more time on our hands to be at home and to have fun with them. What a mismatch! For we gaze at their tidy but unlived-in rooms with toys neatly stacked that have long since ceased to be in current use. Nevertheless, their possessions are sentimentally kept to remind us of times past and to remind them of their childhood and maybe to be passed on to their children. We wait for their telephone calls or letters or visits. The shoe is now on their foot, not ours. They initiate, we respond.

I was an only child and I dearly loved my parents. But I only got to know my father when I was 37 and he was 70. During my school years from 1952 to 1963 and thereafter at university until 1966, I seldom saw my father. This was partially due to my being at boarding school, but even during the holidays his occupation as a stockbroker meant that he left the house before 7 am and only got back after 7 pm. By the time, as a senior partner of the firm, he had graduated to taking a later train up to London and an earlier train back in the evening, I had moved out of the house.

Yet he was always there when I needed to show off to someone a bit – at cricket matches and the like. And when I started going back to England from here more frequently in the 1980s, we had seven magic years of walking the dog down country lanes and talking about business adult to adult. That's when I really got to know him. Just before he died in October 1987, I had started doing the "High Road" lectures around South Africa. He was genuinely pleased – if not somewhat surprised – at the popularity of the material.

So it goes from generation to generation. I remember witnessing my son take a blinder of a catch at square leg at his preparatory school in a second eleven cricket match. He put his right arm up and the ball which was surely going for a six stuck to his palm. One of the teachers said to me that it was the best catch he'd ever seen. I was very proud but I couldn't do an action replay because I didn't have a video camera. Nevertheless, I still have that miraculous catch in my mind's eye. That's good enough!

No short cuts

To be world class, you have to work hard. There are no short cuts.

13.10.1996 Robert Chamberlain was an undergraduate at Exeter College, Oxford. We would call him a mature student because he arrived there at the age of thirty. He wrote a book called *Nocturnal Lucubrations* while he was taking his degree. To "lucubrate" means to work by artificial light until the early hours of the morning and thereby produce literary compositions by laborious study. Hence, Chamberlain must have occasionally dozed off during his normal daytime lecture programme!

He writes: "It is good for man to be industrious in his youth, and to know that if by honest labour he accomplish any good thing, the labour is soon past, but the good remains to his comfort; and if for his pleasure he do anything that is ill, the pleasure is gone in a moment, but the evil remains to his torment."

Nocturnal Lucubrations was published in 1638. Now let's fast-forward a quarter of a millennium to the 1890s, and switch continents – from Britain to America. John Graham was chairman of Graham and Company, a food firm located in the Union Stock Yards, Chicago. When he was travelling, he used to write letters to his son Pierrepont who also worked for the firm.

His advice to his son is as follows: "Mulligan tells me that you are quick to learn, and that you can do a powerful lot of work when you've a mind to; but he adds that it's mighty seldom your mind takes that particular turn. A man can't have his head pumped out like a vacuum pan, or stuffed full of odds and ends like a bologna sausage, and do his work right. It doesn't make any difference how mean and trifling the thing he's doing may seem, that's the big thing and the only thing for him just then. Business is like oil – it won't mix with anything but business."

He continues: "Once a fellow's got the primary business virtues cemented into his character, he's safe to build on. But when a clerk crawls into the office in the morning like a sick setter pup, and leaps from his stool at night with the spring of a tiger, I'm a little afraid that if I sent him off to take charge of a branch house he wouldn't always be around when customers were. He's the sort of a chap who would hold back the sun an hour every morning and have it gain two every after-noon if the Lord would give him the same discretionary powers that He gave Joshua."

Fast-forward again to the present day. In its obituary on Paul Erdos, one of the finest mathematicians of this century, *The Economist* said that he simply constructed his life to extract from his magnificent obsession the maximum amount of happiness. Erdos himself said that a mathe-matician is a machine for converting coffee into theorems. He liked drinking the stuff.

Despite the large span of years between these three quotations, they convey more or less the same sensible message to young people. Hard work and the feeling you've made a lasting contribution enhance your quality of life in the long term. Contrarily, slacking off or trying to achieve quick-run gains at the expense of others leads a person to bitter memories and despair. The current barrage of books which promote the idea of seven easy steps to success and happiness sound hollow and false by comparison. Short cuts don't exist. You've got to focus and burn the candle at both ends if you want to get on.

Advice to youth
Do you want to appear world class to your great-grandchildren? The incident I most remember about my father occurred after he retired as a successful stockbroker. He took me down to the local village church and proudly showed me the renovated roof and pews. He had become treasurer of the church and parlayed a small cash reserve into a considerable fund using his financial acumen. When I asked him why he took on this task because he had never struck me as being particularly religious, he gave me a wry smile and said: "Just hedging my bets!"

12.1.1997 Whenever I talk to young white people about the future of South Africa, I am inevitably asked by them whether they should go or stay. I am probably an inappropriate person to ask because I would never give a direct recommendation either way. In the end each individual must decide for himself or herself based on his or her own personal circumstances. For example, there is a big difference between leaving South Africa for a better job offered overseas and leaving South Africa because of fear of the future for any one of a number of motives – escaping violent crime, no career prospects because of affirmative action, worry about declining standards in education and health, general anxiety about the state of the country when one's children grow up, etc.

Thus, if I do say anything, it is to draw a distinction between wanting to arrive in a new country and wanting to leave this one. The latter motivation has driven many white South Africans from important positions here, where they made a difference, to utterly mediocre positions overseas where their considerable talents are wasted. In any conversation with such South African emigrés, their frustration is highlighted by the fact that they want South Africa to fail in order to justify their original decision to emigrate. The moment you know this is when they say: "Well, you may have made it over the political hurdle but the economy is collapsing around your ears and you're going to end up like the rest of Africa. If not, AIDS is going to kill you anyway."

Nevertheless, one is always anxious that a constant trickle should not become a flood. Already, a substantial number of the children of directors of South African companies have relocated overseas; and they are still the ones with the best prospects locally. Moreover, the majority of white medical students continue to take the gap having had 70 per cent of their costs of tuition subsidised by the state. It would be hilarious, if it wasn't so tragic, that many of the best and brightest of the Western world's medical specialists had their education paid for by a developing country like South Africa.

So what's the case for staying if you're young, ambitious and white? The answer is that this period of South Africa's history, say 1985 to 2025, will probably end up as the most written-about era ever. In 500 years' time, historians will still be fossicking through all the scraps of evidence to discover how this miraculous transition was initiated and how it was subsequently managed. There's a much greater chance of leaving a footprint which your great-great-grandchildren can boast about if you stay and assist with the transition than if you leave for a comfortable but conventional life elsewhere. Who in future generations will give a fig if you become a slick merchant banker in England, send your sons to Eton and successfully launch your daughter on the debutante circuit? How many gravestones have you come across which bear the epitaph "he grew the company's earnings per share consistently at 15 per cent per anum for 25 years" or "he made a million pounds before he was 35"? Yuppies aren't commemorated.

The situation here is sufficiently fluid for ordinary people to do extraordinary things. Heroic things. Heroism is what people are remembered for, not material success. It will be a shame if young South Africans shun the riskier but infinitely more gratifying opportunity to play a positive role in a unique transformation in exchange for a more pedestrian existence in a more advanced society overseas.

The wheel is still in spin. High Road or Low Road – who knows? But every time a young, talented, educated soul leaves these shores, the chances of winning are diminished. The reverse is also true. If you stay, and you are joined by young, energetic Americans, Asians, Africans, Europeans and other immigrants, winning becomes a near certainty. Then your children will be proud.

Headmasters in Docs
When headmasters come in different disguises, they can fool anyone. In the process, I came across something unusual that South Africa would be world class at producing if it was unbanned.

28.4.1996 The other night I experienced a misunderstanding with a marvellous twist to it. According to the folder that my secretary had given to me, I was due to speak to the South African Headmasters' Association at the Edenvale Community Centre. As I drew into a parking place at the centre, I noticed a battered old Kombi stopping beside me. A man stepped out with a couple of dusty old wine bottles, causing me to speculate on what kind of party was taking place in the centre at the same time as my presentation.

On entering the building, I looked at a notice board which listed the evening's events. Various social activities including a meeting of bee-keepers were displayed but nothing was mentioned about head-masters. Luckily somebody came through the doors who recognised me. He said he was going to the same venue and asked me to follow him.

I walked into a room full of people who at first glance did not appear to be headmasters. One was in shorts, the others were dressed very casually and I was the only one in a suit. Interestingly, some of the prospective audience were in the kind of boots which are all the rage among teenagers these days, prompting me to visualise a new advertising campaign around the theme "Headmasters in Docs". I started chatting to one principal who told me he worked at South African Breweries. This observation made me wonder at how much times have changed – a principal who moonlights at a brewery was not a proposition in my day.

Then the fellow whom I had last seen in the car park joined the throng with his two bottles. He put them on a table in a corner and my eye immediately alighted on many other bottles already residing there – of many shapes and sizes. Wine glasses were also provided. So obviously the headmasters were going to celebrate something either before or after my talk. The bottles were labelled informally like home-made jam, so I wandered over for a closer look. The labels shared one word – "mead".

And then it struck me – I was speaking to the South African Meadmasters' Association. I had mistaken a capital "M" for an "H" on the folder. Since mead is an alcoholic beverage made out of honey, water and yeast, the people around me were mostly beekeepers. Their thick boots were to stop bee stings. I've always associated mead with Celts and Anglo-Saxons but it was also drunk out of the skulls of slain enemies by the ancient Vikings. The instructions for mead manufacture were laid down by King Howel the Great in Wales in the tenth century. Specifically, mead with the addition of spices and herbs such as cloves, ginger, rosemary, hyssop and thyme is called metheglin after the Welsh term "meddiglyn". The latter means "physician" because of the drink's reputed medicinal powers. It was also considered an aphrodisiac. The word "honeymoon" comes from the ancient practice of giving newly married couples a bottle of mead to last for the first lunar month of their marriage.

The sale of mead in South Africa has been banned since 1929 on the grounds that it is detrimental to the health of the people. Interestingly, this ban is relaxed at the annual Rand Show where the public can buy a bottle or two from the honey stand. To me it is ridiculous that mead is singled out for prohibition. Obviously there has to be some form of quality control, but what really makes mead any different to wine or whisky? Lifting the ban could lead to a great opportunity for small business development.

After my talk, I tasted all kinds of mead – sweet, dry, rich, light, spiced, unspiced. Even a mead ale was to be had. I woke up the following morning no worse for wear but still chuckling over the misidentification. Beekeepers and headmasters are poles apart!

Mary Knowling

A world-class country is made up of world-class individuals. We start with Mary and Monde who are painting Grahamstown Cathedral.

30.3.1997 Roll up all you do-it-yourself enthusiasts! Do you want a real challenge? How about putting a new coat of paint on the interior of an entire cathedral? No, don't put your paint brushes and ladders away because you think the order is too tall. The task is currently being accomplished right here in South Africa.

Dr Mary Knowling, a retired GP who is a sprightly seventy plus according to the local press, was recently attending a service in Grahamstown Cathedral. She realised that the wall around the stained-glass window donated by her grandfather needed painting. She approached the Dean and offered to sponsor the painting of the wall, hoping that other beneficiaries would follow suit for all the other walls in the cathedral. A few weeks later the council thanked her profusely for her offer to paint the whole cathedral.

Now this cathedral is no ordinary one. It has the tallest spire in South Africa. It is one of Grahamstown's most prominent landmarks along with Rhodes University, H. C. Galpin's Observatory Museum, the 1820 Settlers National Monument and the Mad Hatter's Tea House in the High Street. Its correct name is the Cathedral of St Michael and St George. It took 128 years to build, from its origins as a parish church in 1824 to the completion of the Lady Chapel in 1952. On Sundays its full ring of eight bells can be heard across the City, summoning the faithful to worship. It has an absorbing array of memorial tablets from Grahamstown's frontier days as well as an imposing rood screen, pulpit and organ. As I entered, I noticed the memorial to Colonel John Graham after whom the town is named and who died relatively young at the age of 42. At least his name lives on.

Returning to Mary, she was somewhat taken aback by the council's response. However, she took the bull by the horns and enlisted

Monde Springbok, who normally tends her garden, together with two of his friends to do the job. Borrowing scaffolding from St Andrew's School, and learning as they went along, they have cleaned the interior sandstone and painted two-thirds of the cathedral. At one stage, Monde suggested that he balance the extension ladder on top of the scaffolding to reach the uppermost vaults. Mary felt this was unwise and so the cathedral at this moment is painted to the top of the arches in the aisles.

She has enlisted professional help to remove a few stained-glass windows which are being painstakingly repaired. The choir stalls, which were handcrafted by black pupils who were taught carpentry by her grandfather, have been restored, while the mosaic in the floor has been scrubbed brilliantly clean by two female helpers. Mary herself has led by example. She climbs the extension ladder with impunity and only once forgot to wedge the legs with the lectern. She came crashing to the floor which put her out of action for a couple of weeks. But she's recovered and in spite of a tin knee as a result of an accident when she was young, she is as agile as ever.

As my wife and I walked around the cathedral last Saturday morning, we were deeply impressed by the devotion and respect that she has for her team and they have for her. Above all, they reminded us of the volunteering spirit that is becoming rarer in today's more acquisitive and selfish society. "I want to finish the job before I die," she said. I know she will and they'll all be blessed for it.

Philip Tobias

Philip Tobias is a world-class palaeontologist who can also offer tips on the future. At issue in this article is whether you have to hit the bottom of the barrel before an improvement in your circumstances happens. The National Party changed direction in the late 1980s before a civil war started. Even with their backs to the wall they managed to read the writing on it. We certainly went nowhere near the bottom of the barrel, which at the time would have been a war-ravaged wasteland. So a sense of crisis can occur before the full extent of the crisis is felt. One paints downside scenarios like the "Low Road" precisely to act as an advance warning system of the dangers of sticking to the status quo. The chances are therefore good that we can join the African renaissance up north before we see the bottom of the barrel in an economic sense down here.

8.6.1997 In my original scenario road show in 1986, I used to tell the story about the frog. I hasten to assure those among my readers who are animal rights activists that I've never tried to verify it. If you put a frog into a saucepan of boiling water, it will immediately jump out and survive. However, if you put the same frog into a saucepan of cold water and gently heat it up, it will be unable to detect the gradual increase in temperature and die. In other words, sudden discontinuities are registered on our radar screen and we quickly take evasive action like the frog. Smooth and gradual change which nevertheless ends up transforming the world over an extended period can be lethal.

The frog analogy was recently confirmed in an unusual context. Will Bernard of SAfm decided to air the topic "the past, present and future" on his morning show. With a touch of originality, he invited Professor Philip Tobias and me to be the panel for listeners' calls. There's nothing like a palaeontologist looking back a few million years and a scenario planner looking forward a few decades to handle the arrow of time. What a fascinating and pleasurable experience it was.

The point that most intrigued me was a reply that Tobias gave to a listener who said that Charles Darwin had been proved wrong because there were too many gaps in the chain to validate his theory of evolution. Tobias rebuffed this conjecture by stating that an abundance of missing links had been discovered. However, he went on to say that Darwin had proposed his theory before the science of genetics had become established. In light of the latest information in this area, the idea that nature evolved to a superior form in a gradualist fashion was incorrect. Rather, cataclysmic events of short duration acted as a bottleneck permitting those species which were lucky enough to have the right DNA to get through but extinguishing all the others. Thus has the process of natural selection worked – by fits and starts in response to sudden environmental shocks. It's the frog all over again.

I chimed in that business and governments tend to react in the same way. In the commercial world, nothing focuses the mind like impending bankruptcy. In the political sphere, a crisis is needed to force policy change. For example, in Africa, the countries which appear to have the greatest clarity of vision are the ones that have already experienced the bottom of the barrel. The penny's dropped. Now they're having their renaissance.

Another thought altogether is raised by Tobias's answer. Up till now, the way nature has coped with environmental uncertainty has been through biodiversity. As a result, some species survive whatever impediments artifical or natural causes throw in their path. Nature is like a conglomerate with a sufficiently wide portfolio of assets to hedge against any eventuality. The problem is that mankind is reducing biodiversity by destroying the natural habitat and replacing it with a specialised range of crops which happen to thrive optimally in today's environment. More than 90 per cent of the world's food is derived from fewer than twenty species of plants. But what if the environment changes in a cataclysmic manner that makes these plants unsuitable to grow? A total wipeout is possible.

Against that, genetic engineering may be our saviour by producing entirely new crops. As Tobias indicated, humans are currently using only about 5 per cent of their mental capacity. Raise that figure to 6 per cent – let's not be greedy – and a solution will be found. After all, the human species has managed to survive on the principle that necessity is the mother of invention. Or, as somebody put it more originally, we're like tea bags: hot water brings out the best in us. Maybe, we are smarter than frogs.

Michael O'Dowd

Michael O'Dowd is a South African with a world-class intellect. Together with Bobby Godsell, he wrote the "High Road" and "Low Road" scenarios in 1985.

9.3.1997 Patti Waldmeir has been getting all the press with her new book *Anatomy of a Miracle*. She sets out to study the "psychology of capitulation" which led the National Party to hand over power to the ANC. Her conclusion is summed up with the words: "In Africa, politics is about power. The attitude of African and Afrikaner to power was like their approach to everything else – straightforward . . . *'n Boer maak 'n plan*: when his back is to the wall, the Afrikaner will look for a way out. He is a survivor."

However, there is another new book which, despite receiving less media acclaim than Waldmeir's, is no less insightful. It is called *The O'Dowd Thesis and the Triumph of Democratic Capitalism* by Michael O'Dowd. He is my predecessor as Chairman of the Anglo American and De Beers Chairman's Fund. The difference between the two books is that whereas Waldmeir's is an analysis in retrospect, O'Dowd's first chapter, entitled "The stages of economic growth and the future of South Africa" was written in 1966. In it he says: "I believe that South Africa will follow the normal pattern of political, social and economic development from minority rule, through a liberal era, to a welfare state, and that in the process the race question will be solved."

In the second chapter, published in 1982, he updates his 1966 views as follows: "There will be no revolution in South Africa and liberalisation in the sense of the diminution of racial discrimination and the reduction of racially determined or other status-based inequality will continue at an increasing rate. In fifteen years' time (1997) South Africa will be significantly more free and more democratic than it is now and there will be far greater approximation to equality of opportunity. I am not predicting that it will be a perfect democracy, nor that the distribution of income will be equal by any particular standard, but it will certainly correlate far less with colour or class origin than it does now."

Not bad, eh! A prophesy is more impressive than a historical record. O'Dowd, nevertheless, would be the first to disclaim the notion of being a prophet. He in fact talks of "pattern recognition" in his introduction. In other words, even in fairly chaotic systems, it is often possible to find patterns that have enough regularity to allow limited degrees of prediction. This is done all the time in weather forecasting. The pattern that O'Dowd identified in 1966 was simple: the more a country developed into a modern industrial state, the more it would reject ideologies that got in the way and the greater the odds that it would turn into a democracy.

So O'Dowd looking into the future comes up with a different answer to Waldmeir looking back into the past. Instead of ascribing the radical change in South Africa to the psychologies of the various actors who took part in the political transition, he is more in line with the famous philosopher Hegel. The latter believed that history has certain rules of the game which force the players to change irrespective of their beliefs and their intentions. A thesis is followed by antithesis which ultimately leads to synthesis before the cycle repeats itself. This determinist view doesn't mean that you can predict every step of process that takes you from A to B – only that B is inevitable. O'Dowd's thesis therefore suggests that there was no capitulation by one side to the other. Everybody had to adjust to the rules.

Tass, Marion and Rochelle
Thanks to Tass, Marion and Rochelle for world-class service.

17.12.1995 As we head for Christmas, I thought I would tell a true story that will uplift the spirit. On Friday, December 8, I had to get up at the unearthly hour of 5:00 am to drive my son to the airport for a 7:00 am flight from Johannesburg to Durban. He was going to the South Coast to join some friends for a postmatric holiday. As he was packing, he casually remarked to his parents that he wasn't quite sure how he was going to get from Durban to Margate. This disclosure considerably added to the normal level of anxiety which parents must feel when their offspring are about to spend an unmonitored fortnight with a gang of their matric friends.

My wife thought we had booked a seat on a coach to take him to

Margate and I assumed mistakenly that he was being picked up by one of the said gang. I vainly looked in my pocket for a coach ticket which the travel agent might have supplied with the air ticket. No such luck. So, on the way to the airport, I told my son to check with "Enquiries" at the Durban end about coaches to Margate.

After dropping him off and bidding him a farewell full of cautionary advice about everything, I realised on my way out of the airport that I had not told him that he shouldn't accept a lift from a stranger in the event of the bus being full. This scenario assumed ever more frightening proportions as I drove along the motorway. As soon as I parked my car, I decided to ring SAA all-hours reservations for a phone number in Durban where I could obtain assistance. Thereafter, at about the same time that my son was taking off, I rang the Airport Company in Durban and spoke to Tass Ally. She advised that there were two buses each weekday to Margate, one which left at 9:30 am and the other at 5:45 pm. She immediately gave me the number of the bus company, Margate Mini Coach. There I made contact with Marion De Deugd who said that my son had not been booked on the morning bus but there were still six seats available. Normally she did not accept bookings on the phone, but she realised my son would not sit around all day at the airport waiting for the afternoon bus. Correctly judging my predicament, she promised to contact the driver on his way to Durban from Margate and request him to reserve a seat for my son. I in turn pledged that he had sufficient cash to pay his fare on boarding the bus.

The booking was quickly confirmed. Now I had the problem of conveying this information to my son who by this time had landed in Durban. I contacted the Airport Company again to page him. Coincidentally, he was at the information desk finding out about buses. Over the phone, I heard Rochelle Ogle at the counter talking to him. As soon as she reverted to me, I told her the young man to whom she'd just spoken was my son and asked her to retrieve him. This she successfully accomplished with a loud cry of "Robert". Thus I completed the mission of getting my son to Margate safely, not only to my relief but much to my wife's as well. The booking in retrospect was crucial since all the other spare seats were snapped up on two prior stops in Durban.

The point I wish to make is that the system worked – clickety click. No bureaucratic inertia. Moreover, the three ladies – Tass, Marion and Rochelle – did more than fulfil their roles competently. They went out of their way to satisfy the customer. Their courteousness made me feel warm and proud to live here. Their example serves to confound all those Afro-pessimists who still think South Africa is going down the tubes. Humbug! We're taking the "High Road".

David Rattray
David Rattray is a world-class narrator.

7.4.1996 Isandlwana. 22 January 1879, the day when 25 000 Zulus armed with assegais and shields annihilated 1 774 British soldiers armed with modern breech-loading rifles and artillery. Depending on your perspective, it was the greatest victory in the history of the Zulu nation or the worst defeat in the annals of the British Empire. Valour and honour were widely apparent on both sides, features which are significantly lacking in today's dirty conflicts where the casualties are mainly unarmed civilians.

On Saturday morning, just over a week ago, my wife and I were part of a small party sitting on the slopes of the sphinx-shaped mountain overlooking the battlefield. We were listening to David Rattray – owner of Fugitives' Drift Lodge – providing an expert and moving description of the battle. I came to the conclusion that two brilliant decisions were made by the Zulus and four blunders were made by the British.

On the Zulu side, the commanders were flexible and open-minded. When a small British scouting party accidentally stumbled on the spot where the main body of the Zulu army was concealed, the Zulus immediately brought forward the moment of confrontation and modified their formations accordingly. Originally, they didn't want to fight on the 22nd because it was bad luck to fight on the day of the dead moon (a solar eclipse). However, with their cover blown, they put that superstition to one side. Secondly, they adopted a tactic called the "horns of the buffalo": attack the enemy from the front but cut off any chances of retreat by encircling them on the left and the right flanks. This manoeuvre was staged over an area of many miles. In other words, the plan, even when it was modified, was well thought out in advance and executed with great discipline.

The British, on the other hand, were caught completely off guard. The leader of the military expedition, Lord Chelmsford, split his resources at the worst possible moment by taking the majority of soldiers in the Isandlwana camp on a wild-goose chase. He was looking for the impis in the wrong hills. He didn't even participate in the battle, only arriving back when it was over.

Secondly, he left the camp unfortified because it was temporary and he didn't envisage a scenario of the enemy attacking while he was away. He was just too complacent. Thirdly, he didn't leave a clear chain of command behind at the camp. There were two chief executives during the course of the battle with mutually exclusive strategies. Lt Col Durnford took a force of men to strengthen and extend the line of soldiers who were located at some distance from the camp. Lt Col Pulleine wanted to concentrate his troops close to the camp site. The result was a further division of an already fragmented force.

Lastly, a more general flaw was the British Cabinet giving too much free rein to local administrators in Natal. The campaign was never properly authorised. The absence of modern telecommunications was partially to blame for this. But despatches containing crucial information were deliberately delayed so that a *fait accompli* could be presented to London.

As I looked down on the little piles of white rock which marked where soldiers of the 24th Regiment had fallen, I couldn't help feeling immense pity for them. I pictured those little squares of Welshmen in their scarlet uniforms far from the green hills of home. I saw them fasten their bayonets for the last time with the Zulu cry of "Usuthu" ringing in their ears. They didn't precipitate the war. The politicians did so by foolishly misjudging the pride and the might of the Zulu nation. But, as the old adage goes, politicians make war: soldiers fight them.

CR

CR is a world-class business leader – old and new!

5.5.1996 Looking at the photograph of Cyril Ramaphosa on the front page of the souvenir edition of *Sowetan Business*, I was struck by similarities to another great man with the initials CR – Cecil Rhodes. The quote attributable to Ramaphosa – "I was in the business of politics, now I'm entering the politics of business" – could easily, if reversed, have been said by Rhodes in 1890. That was the year he moved from the world of business to become Prime Minister of the Cape Colony.

Just as it is very rare for a sportsman to be chosen to represent his country at more than one national sport, so it is exceptional that a person climbs to the top of the ladder in politics as well as business. But the two men – Rhodes and Ramaphosa – have much in common.

Firstly, they both rose to the pinnacle of their occupations at absurdly young ages. They were handling immense power when most other people are still consolidating the first phase of their careers and aspiring to rise from junior to middle management. Rhodes had established De Beers Consolidated Mines Limited in Kimberley, the Gold Fields of South Africa Company in Johannesburg and the British South Africa Company to develop the new territory to the north of South Africa by the time he was 35. Ramaphosa had formed the National Union of Mineworkers by the time he was 30 and had played a key role in the formulation of the interim constitution by the time he was 39. He will have supervised the even more important task of drafting a final constitution before he is 44. By his deeds so far, Ramaphosa's name will as assuredly feature in history books about the development of South Africa in the twentieth century, as Rhodes's will continue to feature in books about the previous century.

Rhodes was the consummate deal maker of his era, as is evidenced by the way he progressed from being an impoverished digger to the leader of the diamond industry in a few brief years. He wheeled and dealed until he had everyone under a single umbrella. Ramaphosa has had to cope with a bewildering array of individuals with competing political interests and weld them together into a team with deadlines to meet. He has succeeded extremely well despite the tenseness of having to sort out the thorniest issues in the last lap of the negotiation process.

During a casual conversation when I first met Ramaphosa as general secretary of the NUM, he said to me: "You know, Clem, whenever we have a chat like this, it's bound to end up in some type of negotiation." It demonstrated the single-mindedness of the individual. But then he gave one of those full-bellied laughs which charm the pants off the people he is negotiating with. He is sensationally good at instinctively guessing at his opponent's bottom line, taking him to the brink with a suitable dose of histrionics and then settling just before a dispute is declared. He keeps his word too.

Ramaphosa is his own man, with ambitions that set him apart from his colleagues. When everyone expected him to take a cabinet post in the Government of National Unity, he become ANC secretary-general and chairman of the Constitutional Assembly. Smart move – he added more value his way. Likewise, Rhodes must have exasperated some of his fellow directors because he never regarded moneymaking as an end in itself. His dream of "painting the map red" and building a railway from Cape to Cairo demonstrated a much grander vision than a normal businessman would have.

I can only wish Ramaphosa the best of luck in his new role. As he puts it: "I believe that the ultimate survival of big companies, and of the corporate sector, in this country revolves around how we empower the disadvantaged. If we don't develop clear strategies, we could all lose." He's right. Leaders of business must dedicate themselves to spreading a passion for business among the masses. Business must be easily accessible, not a privileged pastime. We've had a Club for too long. It must disband. And by the beginning of the new century, we need a black equivalent of Rhodes to give everybody a dream. With Ramaphosa, anything is possible.

The Vaid family

The Vaid family are better known at Hardy's in London than Gary Player and Chris Barnard. They sell world-class fishing tackle in Dullstroom.

23.6.1996 While the Cape was reeling under mighty storms last weekend, my family was enjoying three crisp, wintry, clear-blue-sky days that the Highveld is famous for. We were staying in Dullstroom, a small village halfway between Belfast and Lydenburg in Mpumalanga. At this time of year, the golden colour of the rolling hills surrounding Dullstroom contrasts with the steely grey waters of the numerous trout dams which nestle between them.

"Gauties" have discovered Dullstroom, as a ribbon of new developments along the main road through the village attests. Up the hill there's a dairy which has been converted into a pub and further down lie restaurants, tea houses and a shopping mall selling all kinds of nick-nacks. Critchley Common, a residential development consisting of stone cottages clustered around the original lodge, is at the bottom of the hill.

But the real gems are reserved for the tourist who, when heading towards Lydenburg, turns left into the old village at the petrol station in the dip. The Dullstroom Inn is a charming old-style country hotel with a shop next to it that sells lovely tartan caps. Across the road is a turn-of-the-century church with a superb wooden ceiling, pulpit and pews. Everywhere grow oaks and planes and, rarely seen anywhere else, copper beeches. The jewel in the crown, though, is to be found when one passes the hotel and turns left up Slagtersnek Street which runs parallel to the main road. At the top on the right is "The Blue Shop", alternatively known as "The Old Firm" because it has been in existence for eighty years and is further known as "E.M. Vaid & Co." after the family that runs it.

It is probably the best known trout tackle shop in the country. Yet it sells a wide range of general goods as well. The shop was opened in 1916 by Ebrahim Vaid who arrived from India in 1908 with his family. Known as "Rooibaard" due to a beard of legendary red colour, Ebrahim ran a successful general dealers' store. It was his son, Yousuf or Joe to his customers, who added fly-fishing equipment to the shop's range 35 years ago when farmers started stocking their dams with trout which they bred in the cold mountain streams. Joe and his son Mahmood, who both look after the store now, are experienced fly-fishermen themselves. So with any sale goes expert advice on how one should balance the rod with the reel and the line, how one should attach the leader to the line and the fly to the leader. And then of most concern to the client, they offer inside information on the type of flies currently attracting the trout. In the last regard, they can draw from a stock of 608 patterns, 54 000 flies in all. One special fly that Joe has made up himself is called "Cyril's Choice". It bears a close resemblance to the ANC colours and it is used for catching big fish!

They have a "full house" of equipment on offer from starter kits for kids for a few hundred rand to the very best from the House of Hardy for up to R5 000. A lovely story is of the Johannesburger who some years ago visited Hardy's in London and said to the salesman behind the counter: "I come from South Africa, the land of Gary Player and Chris Barnard." To which the salesman replied: "I'm sorry, sir. I'm not familiar with those names but in your country I do know Mr Vaid of Dullstroom who is the largest purveyor of Hardy equipment in the southern hemisphere."

So, in its way, "The Blue Shop" is a world-class establishment. How many other large chains – let alone individual stores – have lasted eighty years? So, for the keen anglers from Natal and the Cape, a true delight awaits you in Dullstroom if you haven't already been there.

Ken Owen

Owen was a world-class columnist. I wish he'd make a comeback.

30.6.1996 To write a weekly column, you have to be disciplined and enthusiastic. Disciplined in the sense of converting ideas into concrete articles of a certain length and by a certain time. Enthusiastic in that you really want to convey a message each week to your readers with freshness and humour such that they will keep coming back for more.

Why am I saying this? Because one of South Africa's most talented and most read columnists is retiring this week – Ken Owen who was editor of the *Sunday Times*. Over the years he has consistently espoused a set of liberal values which are now very much in vogue among those who produce league tables measuring the relative economic performance of nations.

Take the *Global Competitiveness Report* issued two weeks ago by the World Economic Forum based in Geneva. In order of precedence, the list of the top ten nations goes as follows: Singapore, Hong Kong, New Zealand, the US, Luxembourg, Switzerland, Norway, Canada, Taiwan and Malaysia. Now I know that classic liberals might contest that one or two of these countries have not yet developed into proper liberal democracies and there is unnecessary curtailment of press freedom too. But the liberal chestnuts of a strong work ethic, a high savings rate, strong private-sector investment, a predisposition towards free trade and private property ownership and the belief that governments should encourage business but not try and do it themselves are shared by all these countries. Moreover, the report says that "the European Union is slipping behind many parts of the world in economic competitiveness. The current social-welfare system is proving too heavy a fiscal burden." Germany, for example, has slipped from No. 6 to No. 22 (behind Thailand, Chile and Korea).

Another recently published study entitled *Economic Freedom of the World 1975-1995*, written by James Gwartney et al. and sponsored by the Fraser Institute of Vancouver and the Liberty Fund of Indianapolis, delivers the same results. It examined freedom, growth and incomes in 103 countries. The principal message is simple. Countries with the highest level of economic freedom grew at 3,3 per cent per annum per capita over the twenty-year period while those with the lowest level of economic freedom grew at minus 1,3 per cent per annum per capita. Top of the table in this case was Hong Kong followed by New Zealand, Singapore, the US and Switzerland. Bottom were Brazil, Nicaragua, Syria, Algeria, Iran and Zaïre. South Africa was just a little more than halfway down the table at 54th.

But if you think that I'm merely quoting liberal think-tanks in a selective way to support liberal conclusions, how about this. *The New Statesman* of 14 June, a British left-of-centre journal, carried an article by Martin Jacques who was formerly editor of *Marxism Today*. It is called "Tigers and Chameleons". In it he says that Asia's tiger economies have much to teach us about the role of the state. Let me quote him directly: "For a start, we are talking about a small state. In South Korea government spends a mere 16,2 per cent of GDP, in Taiwan and Hong Kong 16, in Singapore 20, while Malaysia is the highest with 25 per cent. This compares with our own 42, Germany's 49 and France's 55 per cent. In the US the figure is 36 per cent and in Japan 33. The explanation for the small state is simple: government in East Asia assumes few of the social responsibilities that we take for granted in Europe and taxation is commensurately low."

Ken Owen is retiring from his job just when the mainstream economic intelligentsia are saying that he was correct all along. How satisfying – for him and Adam Smith!

Rojâne and Matthew

Teach your children well to use their talent.

28.9.1997 What goes around comes around. Rojâne Chivers teaches mathematics at Freeway Park Primary School in Boksburg. In late 1994, she listened to a radio programme in which I was extolling the virtues of small business. Then she picked up a magazine over the Christmas holidays in Cape Town which had an article on the entrepreneurial programme developed for the girls at the Wykeham Collegiate in Pietermaritzburg. In February 1995, she heard from a friend that I had once again spoken at St Alban's College in Pretoria on the need to create a new entrepreneurial class.

So she said she was inspired to say to her pupils in March 1995: "I have a dream. Would you like to start your own businesses?" She left it at that until the pupils gave her a gentle reminder in September: "Where is your dream? Have you forgotten about it?" This precipitated her to draw on the experience she had at the Trinity Methodist Church in Boksburg. Each member of the congregation received a loan of R10 from the church and was told to make it grow in accordance with the scriptures. Remember the story of the talents in St Matthew 25: how a couple of the servants doubled what they'd been given, while the third told his master he'd sat on his talent for fear of retribution if he lost it. His master immediately admonished him and gave his talent to one of the other two with words which sound remarkably capitalistic: "For, unto every one that hath shall be given, and he shall have abundance: but from him that hath not shalt be taken away even that which he hath. And cast ye the unprofitable servant into outer darkness: there shall be weeping and gnashing of teeth."

Rojâne took up the challenge and persuaded the school to lend R10 to each child. There were 120 children in the four Standard 4 classes she taught, so the school laid out a total sum of R1 200. She enlisted the help of sixteen dads and mums to be mentors with the idea that the kids would have a minimarket a month later in the school grounds on a Friday afternoon. The stalls offered food like hot dogs, cold drinks, pancakes and candy floss; gifts like Christmas cards, pens and caps; and games to play like skittles and darts. Each child had to hire a table for R1 and they were charged an extra R1 if their table wasn't spick and span.

The market was expected to last an hour and a half but was overwhelmed by customers and operated from 1.45 pm to 8 pm. Receipts amounted to R7 200 of which R1 200 went back to the school for repayment of the loan, R600 went to the PTA as a share of the surplus and R500 went to various charities. The children kept the balance of R4 900. Safe to say, the outcome far exceeded expectations.

In 1996 the loan was upped to R20 per pupil. At the same time, Rojâne changed the rules of the game because she felt the 1995 function had been run more like a fete than a commercial market. Parents were therefore discouraged from making significant donations of goods to their children's stalls. Under this stricter regimen, the market took in about R7 400 of which R2 400 was used to repay the loan, R500 went to the PTA, R650 was allocated to the Standard 5 farewell party and the kids pocketed R3 850. Like the servants with their talents, the profit per individual pupil varied considerably from zero to R500. This year, instead of a compulsory donation to the Standard 5 party, part of the profit is to be committed beforehand to printing a flier advertising the event. This is to promote the concept that something has to be ploughed back into the business for it to expand. It was a marvellous story she told me when I met her in person recently. I am now using it as an example of the kind of breakthrough a world-class spirit of innovation can achieve. Kids can be taught to be entrepreneurs, even at the tender age of eleven and twelve.

Peter Knipp
If you listened to Peter, he would have you eating out of the palm of his hand.

14.9.1997 Sometimes one hears a humdinger of a speech on the most unlikely topic. Such was the case at the Cape Gourmet Festival at Spier this year. The speaker was Peter Knipp, until recently Executive Chef of Raffles Hotel in Singapore, and his topic "Food and Beverages: Fact or Fiction?"

He kicked off with the money factor – it makes the world spin around, no point avoiding it. Contrary to the belief of many practitioners in the culinary arts, it is not a dirty word. Indeed, it is the basic principle of existence in business. Great restaurants can make money, though most are more interested in "face value", i.e. the image they present to clients. So, the idea persists in the profession that a good restaurant doesn't have to make a healthy profit as long as it keeps its name. This flies in the face of the fact that owners nowadays are expecting healthy returns on their investments. Actually, when you look into it, personal egos and badly planned outlets are responsible for poor financial performance. The excuse of offering excellent food and service at bargain prices has nothing to do with it.

By and large, hotels with poor food and beverages (F&B) fall into two categories. Either they regard F&B as a marginal activity because it is much harder to make money out of F&B than rooms. In rooms, you only have to move the position of the soap occasionally, whereas F&B demands greater originality. Mediocre management therefore view it as a burdensome service as opposed to a profit centre (remember Basil's attitude in the BBC's *Fawlty Towers*).

Alternatively, a complacent manager thinks that his hotel has such a great name that it doesn't really matter if the F&B is pretty indifferent. The guests will still come. But hotels with outstanding F&B like Raffles in Singapore, the Oriental in Bangkok and Vier Jahreszeiten in Hamburg have developed their in-house restaurants and bars as separate entities which maximise their own potential. In the main bar at Raffles, total costs including drinks, bartenders' salaries and rent amount to only 10 per cent of the takings. That's profitable.

So what is the schedule of action for success in F&B? Evaluate the market concisely. Money well spent on surveys can save and make millions. Establish a definitive direction for your outlet by analysing and choosing the right concept. Menus with a little bit of everything always fail. Don't overlook local food. One Californian proprietor gave the order: "Out with the frog legs. In with our own recipes." He is such a success that the French copy him now. Eliminate personal favourites like silver cutlery in favour of satisfying customers' real needs. Gather these plus feedback on your own performance by asking clients what they did and more importantly didn't like about the meal before they walk out of the door. However, don't change direction without having made a proper analysis of any of their objections. Particularly beware of personal but trivial comments from influential people deflecting you from the right path.

Treat F&B as fluid and evolutionary. Never be satisfied with short-term successes. Be on the constant lookout for things which improve long-term potential. Certainly, don't expect short cuts to yield big results. Spend part of your time evaluating the competition by eating in their restaurants so you know where to focus your own niche. Don't expect miracles from badly selected staff who are paid peanuts. Little in, less out. Only hire the best and remunerate them well. Accord equal attention to the front and the back of the house alike.

Have effective cost control systems in place. Treat each cost component separately and don't cover one poor area by making the better ones subsidise it. Make each manager accountable but prevent him or her from being excessively financially driven as this usually leads to disaster. Have a sound relationship between time spent on cost control and running the operation. Never compromise unless you have carefully evaluated the downside.

In the final analysis, a well-executed F&B operation will not only have an outstanding name but be a financial success – a win-win situation. Peter Knipp not only has a delicate touch with dishes, he could be a brilliant manager of anything with the sage advice he offers.

Twentieth-century heroes and villains
Here is my list of world-class heroes and villains of the twentieth century for what it's worth.

22.9.1996 A couple of weeks ago, columnist George Will raised a fascinating concept in *Newsweek*: "Man of the Century" based not on morality, but impact. His choice was Lenin because one can trace to him two of the twentieth century's defining ideas: totalitarianism founded on terror; and genocide as state policy. He adds: "From Baghdad to the remnants of Yugoslavia, there are a lot of little Lenins out there, practising in public what he preached in private."

My rogues' gallery would, unlike Will, feature Hitler in pole position with Stalin and Mao Tse-tung following close behind. Though the last two murdered more people, Hitler was more evil and had more impact in a way that he didn't intend. The world was so revolted by what he did in the name of creating a master race that egalitarianism and nonracism

165

have become unassailable principles since the end of World War II. Hence, all ideologies which contradict these two principles have been chucked out including colonialism and apartheid. This has created a very different world.

Nevertheless, one must not overlook the fact that there are plenty of good people who have had a sensational impact. Moreover, I think we should widen the title to "Person of the Century". In a political dimension, Emily Pankhurst, a suffragette who got women the vote and so began the process of their empowerment, features high on my list. Martin Luther King, who changed the face of the most powerful nation on Earth, the United States, also attracts my support. Churchill and Ghandi would be the only political leaders I'd choose and maybe Gorbachev for setting in motion the transition of Russia. The title of freedom-fighter of the century would go to Che Guevara.

In nonpolitical areas, the most obvious one to look at is science. Logie Baird with the television, Bell with the telephone (although one might have to count him out since he made the discovery in 1876), Einstein with "$E = mc^2$" which led to the atomic age, Bohr with the development of quantum physics all have to be considered. However, medicine might carry the day on the grounds that it is responsible for the population explosion we are currently experiencing. Fleming with the discovery of penicillin would be my favourite in this field.

In business, Henry Ford stands out for introducing the technique of mass production. But for legacies that will last into the new century, Bill Gates is an obvious candidate for popularising the personal computer, as is Ted Turner for founding CNN. Religion has notably few people in the running. Maybe Billy Graham, but if I were to choose a name it would be the Ayatollah Khomeini for the resurgence of Islam.

Outside science, literature has been relatively barren of really powerful books which have changed human thought in the last 96 years. My own preference would be someone like Dr Spock, because he has had such an influence – for better or worse – on the way children are now brought up. In music, I'd definitely go nonclassical and choose Lennon and McCartney, and possibly Presley for ushering in rock 'n roll. In art, well, Picasso. In films and theatre, Laurence Olivier would be hard to beat but I would supplement his name with Greta Garbo as a legend and Meryl Streep for acting skill. Finally, as regards sport, my list would include Pele, Bradman, Meads, Nicklaus and Muhammad Ali.

Inevitably, this article is highly subjective, and contains important exclusions. But it is a challenging subject to think about when we're so close to the end of the century.

A special villain called Pol Pot
Pol Pot has a special place in my list of world-class villains too.

7.5.1995 Some photographs leave me haunted and angry. This time it's a dozen of them – black-and-white portraits in the 17 April edition of *Time*. They contrast sharply with gorgeous supermodel Claudia Schiffer and her blonde tresses on the cover of the magazine.

One portrait is of a mother impassively holding a sleeping baby. The baby's head appears in the bottom left-hand corner of the frame as though it is incidental to the photograph. Another portrait is of a serene young girl in what looks like a school uniform buttoned up at the collar. But the collar is untidily crumpled at the back of her neck. A third portrait is of an old man with eyes tightly closed in fear and the number 78 on his chest. A middle-aged woman with her lips pursed and a teenager, arms strapped behind her back and the number 3 pinned to her jacket, make up the fourth and fifth snapshots. Numbers 108 and 8 follow, both men with piercing pupils and wide mouths, dressed in denim. A young soldier in his helmet comprises the eighth portrait.

The last four are young boys – numbers 1, 17, 186 and number unknown – one has bruises around his puffy eyes while the other has a disfiguring gash on his left cheek. The third has a huge bandage on his right cheek while the fourth is unmarked down to his naked shoulders. Twelve photographs of nameless people, that *Time* has put in a centrefold. None of them are smiling, unlike Claudia's provocative pout on the cover. This is hardly surprising since these people were scheduled to be tortured and executed shortly after the photographs were taken. *Time's* caption reads "Faces from the Grave".

A macabre anniversary fell on 16 April. It was the day the Khmer Rouge entered Phnom Penh twenty years ago. That was the beginning of Pol Pot's crazy scheme to send all Cambodians out to the countryside to labour in the fields. They came to be known as the "killing fields" in memory of the million or so people who died in the experiment. Anyone resisting the revolution was sent to secret prisons like Tuol Sleng, code-named S-21. Before being inhumanly despatched, each "treasonous" individual was photographed for posterity. Normally, when one dwells on the mindless cruelty of the Khmer Rouge, one thinks of rows of gleaming white skulls discovered in mass graves. Here were twelve faces of twelve individual members of the human race which presumably joined that collection of skulls.

Quite rightly, Hitler is seen as the epitome of evil in this century. The fiftieth anniversary of the Holocaust, in which six million Jews were killed, fell on our Freedom Day – 27 April. But there are other beasts on a cosmic scale – Pol Pot is one of them. Whenever a megalomaniac elevates race, the state, power or a pet ideology above the value of human life, a crime against humanity is in the offing. Seeing those twelve photographs reminds me of the following lines of a 1960's ballad: "Where have all the flowers gone, long time passing? Where have all the flowers gone, long time ago? Where have all the flowers gone, gone to graveyards every one. When will they ever learn? When will they every learn?" *Time* was correct to mark the anniversary of a less well-known but shameful event in such a shocking way. Will we never learn?

FDR and Maggie Thatcher
I like crunchy leaders like FDR and Maggie Thatcher.

27.10.1996 I've always associated Franklin D. Roosevelt, arguably the greatest US president of this century, with "big government". His span of office covered the Great Depression of the 1930s and World War II of the 1940s. He was responsible for the New Deal in America, a series of government-sponsored programmes in the countryside and the cities to alleviate the suffering of the general populace caused by the 30s depression. It was breathtaking in scale and brought a new meaning to the world "liberal". Up till then the word had retained its classical flavour of "laissez faire" but thenceforward the meaning was widened to cover caring government, i.e. one that helps people and communities to help themselves.

However, an excellent article by Arthur Schlesinger, Jr in *Newsweek* casts a new perspective on FDR's contribution. Contrary to popular opinion, the essence of FDR's approach was a belief in experiment. "The country needs," FDR said in 1932, "and, unless I mistake, the country demands, bold persistent experimentation. It is common sense to take a method and try it. If it fails, admit it frankly and try another. But above all, try something." In other words, failure does not mean "wrong". It means "try again". All great breakthroughs are achieved after going up blind alleys. Innovation is preceded by frustration and pain.

As a challenger of conventional wisdom, FDR knew that he would induce a hostile reaction from entrenched interests. "Judge me," he said to the people, "by the enemies I have made." Before FDR, Alexis de Tocqueville wrote that "democratic eras are periods of experiment, innovation and adventure" but added as a caution "I cannot but fear that men may arrive at such a state as to regard every new theory as a peril, every innovation as an irksome toil, every social improvement as a stepping-stone to revolution, and so refuse the move altogether for fear of being moved too far". In modern parlance, de Tocqueville feared paralysis by analysis – a scourge that afflicts many faint-hearted bureaucracies today.

I wish FDR's words would ring in our government's ears. Not, I hasten to say, that they should copy FDR's policies. These were designed for a different world at a different time. He had to deal with unemployment created by the exodus of people out of agriculture into manufacturing and by the downward spiral in international trade. Now we have to live with unemployment caused by global competition and the transition from large-scale manufacturing to smaller-scale service industries.

Nevertheless, the principle of boldness is correct. If our government wants to tackle head-on the overriding problem of social exclusion, they have to think radically about what initial conditions will lead to an entrepreneurial chain reaction in this country. How do we get everybody to wheel and deal? Then they must go for it, irrespective of ill feelings from those left behind, and turn their ideas into action. The late Nico Colchester, former deputy editor of *The Economist*, put it very well: "Crunchiness brings wealth. Wealth leads to sogginess. Sogginess brings poverty. Poverty creates crunchiness. From this immutable cycle we know that to hang on to wealth, you must keep things crunchy."

FDR was crunchy: so was Maggie Thatcher. New Zealand is crunchy. Unfortunately, we're both soggy and poor at the moment. The discouraging "yes but" syndrome which kills ideas when they are still in bud must give way to a positive climate for experimentation and innovation. We have had transition: now we need transformation. Transformation is never perfect. It is bound to go in fits and starts.

Princess Di
As you can see, I'm a Di fan.

26.11.1995 Oh boy! Those eyes and that shy smile from a head that is slightly arched forward. She really is beautiful. To me, Princess Diana rated ten out of ten in her interview on BBC's *Panorama* programme with Martin Bashir.

People talk of the glamorous Princess, but the word "glamorous" does not suit her. Hollywood starlets are glamorous, but they don't interview like Princess Diana. She has an inner as well as an outer beauty. She has soul, she has heart and she articulates her emotions and experiences in that typically clipped upper-class British manner which steers clear of cloying sentimentalism.

In this respect, her best quote during the interview was: "I'm not a political animal, but I think the biggest disease this world suffers from in this day and age is the disease of people feeling unloved. And I know I can give love – for a minute, for half an hour, for a day, for a month – I can give, and I am very happy to do that."

Her outstanding ability lies in practising what she preaches, as she tours hospitals for lepers and AIDS sufferers and gives them a hug, lights up charity functions with her radiant smile and greets crowds in such a way that everyone feels a personal contact with the Princess. She does the job superbly, better than anyone else in the Royal Family. In fact, she has made the Royal Family relevant to the needs of a modern society by genuinely adding value in areas that politicians cannot. No President, no Premier, no Prime Minister can emulate her mystique, with the possible exception of our own President. She inspires ordinary people to be extraordinary, to go that extra mile in whatever endeavour they're involved in. She is worth every cent she is paid out of the state coffers.

And yet her private life – apart from being an obviously doting mother of her two boys, William and Harry – is a mess. As she says in the interview, the higher you rise in media terms, the further you fall. Her bulimia, her attempts to injure herself, her affairs as she became estranged from her husband have all received millions of column inches. Yet she has won sympathy and understanding from the vast majority out there because, as she puts it: "I take some responsibility that our marriage went the way it did. I'll take half of it, but I won't take any more than that. Because it takes two to get in that situation." In other words, she is not altogether to blame.

I guess the interview was so mesmerising because she demonstrates the same contrasting qualities – of calm and rage, common sense and unreasonableness, resolution and vulnerability – that most of us possess. She is human. Like all of us, she has been through cycles of joy and despair. Like us, she can enjoy good company or be awfully alone. But meanwhile she has made an immense contribution to humanity even though she is still only 34 years old. Let's hope she continues to do so.

Tom Peters
Tom is a world-class business guru who lives his life out loud.

28.1.1996 I had the pleasure last Monday of opening and closing a presentation by Tom Peters at the Carlton Hotel in Johannesburg. He is the foremost business evangelist in the world and with Bob Waterman wrote the best-selling business book ever *In Search of Excellence*. South Africans on the whole are passionate about politics and sport. They're not passionate about business. In contrast, Tom portrays business as a cooperative activity that can be incredible fun and the best adventure for anyone to experience in his or her lifetime.

This dovetails with a point I make in my "High Road" lectures. Being world class in rugby and cricket is all very well, but it is not the ultimate determinant of a country's long-term fortunes. Being world class in business is. Not even politics is more important. Do you associate the Swiss more closely with their cantons or their watches, the Japanese with the quality of their prime ministers or their cars? Democracy is a necessary but not a sufficient condition for a winning nation. Now for some of Tom's pearls of wisdom gleaned from a multiplicity of sources.

The only sustainable advantage for a company comes from out-innovating the competition. But incrementalism is innovation's worst enemy, sanity is the playground of the unimaginative. Most of the world's great innovators are crazy; if they were to pitch up at most companies' personnel departments looking for a job, they'd be flatly turned down. Innovators lead markets, they don't follow them. When society was in a state of wheel-lessness, who wanted the wheel? It was probably a flop to begin with, like video cassette recorders and cellular telephones. Curious corporations employ curious people – ones who have gaps in their CVs.

If you can't say why you've made your company a better place, you're out. Management by objectives and performance appraisal should be replaced by all employees having to do annual resumes in which they show not only how they have added value to the company but how they have improved themselves. Customers must testify to the truth of these resumes.

Companies should have a bias for action. Instead of Ready, Aim, Aim, Aim . . . it should be Ready, Fire, Aim. It is not new ideas that get companies into trouble, it is old ideas that they won't forget. Occasionally, one needs strategic forgetfulness.

Forget the boss. While working in a restaurant as a student, Tom saw himself as CEO and Entertainer-in-Chief of his five tables and fifteen seatings and 38 guests between 5.30 and 11 each night. And nobody could stop him. Let no one complain that they can't make something out of even the humblest job. The express aim of one hotel is that the housekeepers on each floor should see themselves as Michelangelos in keeping the rooms beautifully clean. After all, customers see more of them than the manager and are directly affected by the quality of their work. Companies should put the person who serves the customer first – and the customer second.

What creates trust, in the end, is the leader's manifest respect for followers. Outstanding companies spend 6 per cent of gross revenue on training. Conversely, 70 per cent of people interviewed as to why they switched to a competitor in a particular industry did so because of bad contact with their original supplier's staff (nothing to do with product). In a recent review of the American car industry, the most defective area was customer service.

Tom's best story was how at a conference he was asked by one of the audience what relevance his ideas on customer service could be if a business was self-service. He gave an inadequate response. After the presentation, he was approached by the owner of a petrol station who said he could have given a much better answer. His business was situated at a busy junction with three rival stations in close proximity. He offered self-service which had successfully drawn business away from his three competitors. He filled the cars himself, cleaned the windows himself and vacuumed the interiors himself! Even though his competitors saw him doing this, they did not follow suit. Wrongly they thought that differentiation lay in the chemical additives in the petrol. They were blind to the fact that simple things count.

Tom, you're welcome back any time. To use your lingo, for a 53-year-old you live your life out real loud. You are a true dispenser of enthusiasm. Maybe Nelson Mandela should twist your arm to do a one-month road show for free so that next time everyone can get to hear your passionate message – and have their molecules rearranged.

Andrew Wiles

In reviewing the mathematical thriller Fermat's Last Theorem *I encountered the ferocious concentration of a world-class mathematician. Intense focus works in any context. Take the current trend of larger companies outsourcing their noncore activities to smaller companies. Because the "surplus" activities are the bread and butter of the smaller group, they give them complete attention and therefore do them better.*

5.10.1997   An astronomer, a physicist, and a mathematician (it is said) were holidaying in Scotland. Glancing from a train window, they observed a black sheep in the middle of a field. "How interesting," observed the astronomer, "all Scottish sheep are black!" To which the physicist responded, "No, no! *Some* Scottish sheep are black!" The mathematician gazed heavenward in supplication, and then intoned, "In Scotland there exists at least one field, containing at least one sheep, *at least one side of which is black.*"

This story originally appeared in Ian Stewart's *Concepts of Modern Mathematics*. It is an illustration of mathematicians' zeal for logical rigour and absolute truth, a characteristic which sets them apart from normal mortals. The story was repeated in *Fermat's Last Theorem*, a stubby little unputdownable book by Simon Singh, published in 1997. The book traces the history of how the world's greatest riddle was finally cracked by a British mathematician, Andrew Wiles.

The riddle was originally posed in 1637 by Pierre de Fermat, the French mathematician renowned for being the Prince of Amateurs. While there are innumerable solutions for $x^2 + y^2 = z^2$ (the algebraic notation for Pythagoras' Theorem) there are no solutions for $x^n + y^n = z^n$ where $n = 3$ or any other higher number. In the margin of his copy of Diophantus' *Arithmetica*, he jotted down: "I have a truly marvellous demonstration of this proposition which this margin is too narrow to contain." These words have haunted some of the most brilliant mathematical minds who since then have tried to recreate Fermat's lost proof. That is until Andrew Wiles came along. He worked unrelentingly on the problem for eight years and emerged with a final proof in September 1994. What fascinated me about his long period of travail was that he employed exactly the kind of focus and innovation I have been talking about as conditions for achieving world-class status.

In Singh's book, Wiles recalls: "Sometimes I realised that nothing that had ever been done before was any use at all. Then I just had to find something completely new – it's a mystery where that comes from. Basically it's just a matter of thinking. Often you write something down to clarify your thoughts, but not necessarily. In particular when you've reached a real impasse, when there's a real problem that you want to overcome, then the routine kind of mathematical thinking is of no use to you. Leading up to that kind of new idea there has to be a long period of tremendous focus on the problem without any distraction. You have to really think about nothing but that problem – just concentrate on it. Then you stop. Afterwards there seems to be a kind of period of relaxation during which the subconscious appears to take over and it's during that time that some new insight comes."

On another occasion in the book, Wiles described his lonely odyssey in terms of a journey through a dark unexplored mansion. "One enters the first room of the mansion and it's dark. Completely dark. One stumbles around bumping into furniture but gradually you learn where each piece of furniture is. Finally, after six months or so, you find the light switch, you turn it on, and suddenly it's all illuminated. You can see exactly where you were. Then you move into the next room and spend another six months in the dark. So each of these breakthroughs, while sometimes they're momentary, sometimes over a period of a day or two, they are the culmination of, and couldn't exist without, the many months of stumbling around in the dark that precede them."

The darkest moment of all came after Wiles's initial lecture on his proof in June 1993. A problem with the logic was identified by one of the referees which at one stage looked as if it would destroy the whole foundation of his proof. But Wiles rallied to the challenge and describes the final piece of the puzzle he discovered just over a year later: "It was so indescribably beautiful; it was so simple and so elegant. I couldn't understand how I'd missed it and I just stared at it in disbelief for twenty minutes. Then during the day I walked around the department, and I'd keep coming back to my desk looking to see if it was still there. It was still there. I couldn't contain myself, I was so excited. It was the most important moment of my working life. Nothing I ever do again will mean as much."

In consequence, a riddle that had confounded the world's greatest minds for 357 years was no more.

Campbell and Wilmut

Scotland has always produced world-class scientists. Campbell and Wilmut are the latest in line.

15.6.1997   Send in the clones. Judy Collins didn't quite sing it that way. However, the amended refrain sounds appropriate to celebrate an unusual event which occurred in July 1996: the birth of Dolly. She was named after Dolly Parton, the country-and-western singer unfairly renowned for her bust measurements rather than some of her excellent compositions. In particular, "I will always love you" became a monster hit for Whitney Houston.

There never was another ewe like Dolly. She was the first ever artificially cloned mammal from a single adult cell. Fittingly, she was born in Scotland whence many of the world's greatest scientists have emanated. The two scientists who manufactured Dolly and pushed the frontiers of science forward were Keith Campbell and Ian Wilmut at the Roslin Institute. How did they achieve this stunning breakthrough?

Firstly, they extracted a mammary cell from a Finn Dorset ewe. This cell contains copies of every gene needed to make a sheep. But only those genes needed to reproduce more mammary cells are active. The rest are passive. In this regard, all adult cells are similar: as they mature, they turn into specialists which produce only those cells associated with a specific function in the body.

This is where the genius of the two Scotsmen came into play. They discovered that if a cell is starved of nutrients, it can be stilled at that early moment in its development when all its genes are open to activation. Such is the case in everyday life with identical twins; the original cell divides before it has taken on special tasks. Each half therefore has the ability to grow into a complete being.

The next step for the scientists was to obtain an egg from a Scottish Blackface ewe. The egg was kept alive in a laboratory dish while its nucleus was removed. At this point, the egg was fused with the quiescent mammary cell using a spark of electricity. Molecules in the egg then switched on all the genes in the mammary cell to produce a lamb embryo. The embryo was implanted into a surrogate mother and – bingo – an immaculate conception followed. Dolly emerged into the wide world.

Dolly's birth was announced in a paper in *Nature* at the end of February 1997. She instantly became the most famous sheep in history. This is not because she opened up new methods of rearing sheep. Rather, she brings closer the possibility of cloning a human. Instead of boasting that your child is a chip off the old block, you might one day be able to say that he or she is a chip off the same block. This scenario has been the stuff of fiction for a long time. Aldous Huxley's *Brave New World* first raised the notion of mass producing the human race in a laboratory. The movie *The Boys from Brazil* was based on a plot to clone little Hitlers. More recently *Jurassic Park* was all about cloned dinosaurs and in *Multiplicity* Michael Keaton cloned himself.

However, we're still some way off with the real thing. It's not known if Dolly is an exact genetic duplicate including aspects like temperament. She can't tell us. Moreover, even if you do produce an exact physical replica of yourself, your opposite number will not qualify as an identical individual, because the latter's lifetime experiences and hence stream of consciousness will be different. This condition applies to identical twins. Nevertheless, a US ethics panel set up by President Clinton and comprising eighteen scientists, lawyers and theologians last week recommended that Congress enact legislation to ban the cloning of entire human beings for at least three to five years, but allow the cloning of human embryos for private laboratory research. In other words, scientists could produce cloned embryos but would be prohibited from implanting them into women's wombs to make viable babies. Some form of clone control is therefore on the cards, at least in America.

Meanwhile a company called Valiant Venture Limited, with head-quarters in the Bahamas, has been launched on the Internet with plans to build a laboratory in a country where human cloning is not illegal. It will offer infertile or homosexual couples the chance to have a child cloned from one of them. Never underestimate the power of the market.

Bill Gates

Nobody had ever made $20 billion by the age of forty – until Bill came along. Because of the latest boom in stocks in America, that figure has more than doubled to $42 billion, or close to R200 billion. If you counted R100 notes every second for sixty years, you still wouldn't reach his fortune.

25.2.1996 I've just finished reading Bill Gates's *The Road Ahead*. I enjoyed it immensely because it not only describes how "the information highway will transform our culture as dramatically as Gutenberg's press did in the Middle Ages", it also gives you a clue about why the author is so phenomenally successful and rich.

The first photograph of the book shows a twelve-year-old Gates at Lakeside School in Seattle. He is standing by the door of a room which accommodates the school's computer terminal. He is intently watching his friend Paul Allen, three years older and future co-founder of Microsoft, working at the terminal. In today's computer literate society, this scene would be normal. But back in 1968 kids were out surfing, not playing tick-tack-toe like Gates and Allen on the computer. This early obsession with computers led the two young men to understand the revolutionary implications of a fairly obscure announcement in the summer of 1972 by a young firm called Intel. It was buried on page 143 of *Electronics* magazine and stated that a microprocessor chip called the 8008 was about to be released. Gates and Allen realised that, given the right software, a microprocessor could be transformed from a single instrument like a drum or a horn – good for basic rhythm or uncomplicated tunes – into an accomplished orchestra capable of playing anything. The chip would no longer be condemned to be a beast of burden carrying out simple instructions inside a calculator or elevator, it could itself grow up into a general-purpose computer.

Accordingly, they wrote to Intel who sent them a manual for the 8008. Despite the unsophisticated nature of the chip, they managed to harness its power to measure traffic flows on city streets. They were disappointed that no municipality actually purchased their machine. However, in the spring of 1974, *Electronics* magazine announced Intel's new 8080 chip. Not even the scientists at Intel saw its full potential. To them, the 8080 represented nothing more than an improvement in chip technology. In the short term they were right, but Gates and Allen's dream of a world where a computer was personal, affordable and adaptable was closer to being fulfilled.

Finally the moment arrived after Gates had enrolled at Harvard University and Allen had taken a job nearby at Honeywell in Boston. On a cold Massachusetts morning in January 1975, they bought a copy of *Popular Electronics*. On the cover was a small computer called the Altair 8800. It had no keyboard or display but it did have an 8080 chip as its brain. They wrote the software for the little machine, quit their existing occupations and formed the first microcomputer software company – Microsoft – later in 1975.

The breakthrough that boosted Microsoft into the megacompany league was the launch of the IBM Personal Computer in August 1981. This PC offered three operating systems. One of them was MS-DOS, designed by Microsoft. The genius of Gates and Allen was that besides wanting their product to be the best, they had sufficient foresight to see the IBM PC as an ideal opportunity to establish MS-DOS as the industry standard. So they gave IBM the licence to use their system for a low one-time fee, thereby providing IBM with an incentive to push MS-DOS and to sell it at a low price.

However, Microsoft reserved the right to license MS-DOS to other computer companies that manufactured PCs compatible with the IBM PC. This is where they made their money. They also encouraged other software developers to turn out applications which ran on the MS-DOS platform, notably Lotus 1-2-3. Then came Microsoft's own Windows programme. Now the company has 17 000 employees and around R22 billion a year in sales.

To sum up, Gates is the richest man in the world for two reasons. Firstly, he and his colleague Allen were the first to perceive the true significance of the microprocessor. Secondly, they were prepared to sacrifice financial gain in the short term for wide-spread customer acceptance and much larger commercial benefits in the long term. It was a case of first fame, then fortune.

The Fab Four

The Fab Four were the greatest.

10.12.1995 A poster advertised a garden fete at Woolton Parish Church in Liverpool on Saturday 6 July 1957. The fete was to be opened by Dr Thelwall Jones and included the crowning of the Rose Queen. Also on the programme were the Liverpool Police Dogs Display, the Band of Cheshire Yeomanry and the Quarry Men Skiffle Group. The charge for adults was 6d and for children 3d.

It was an important day in the history of rock music. For that afternoon the leader of the aforementioned skiffle group, John Lennon, met Paul McCartney for the first time. Paul shortly afterwards introduced John to George Harrison, who passed the audition to be the new group's lead guitarist by playing "Raunchy" on the upper level of a double-decker bus. Ringo Starr joined later as a replacement drummer for Pete Best. The Beatles were born. The rest, as they say in show business, is history.

These interesting facts on the origin of the Beatles were revealed in the first part of an enthralling programme entitled *The Beatles Anthology*, screened late on Tuesday night on TV1. Between 1957 and 1962, the Beatles transformed themselves from ordinary rock 'n rollers with ducktails and leather jackets, playing cover versions of "That'll be the day" and "Ain't she sweet", to highly proficient and original musicians. This they did by playing numerous gigs in Liverpool, particularly at the Cavern Club, and by doing a spell in Hamburg. After being turned down by Decca, they started recording for Parlophone. In October 1962, the group had their first national hit with "Love me do". It peaked at No. 17 on the charts. But it served the purpose of spreading their fame beyond Liverpool.

Then The Beatles hit their stride with four singles in 1963 comprising "Please please me", "From me to you", "She loves you" and "I want to hold your hand" – a No. 2 on the charts followed by a hat trick of No. 1s. Beatlemania struck. They were followed everywhere by sighing, shrieking, fainting fans who make today's pop audiences look subdued by comparison. John Lennon at the Royal Variety Performance in November made a memorable quote on stage : "For our last number, I'd like to ask your help. Will the people in the cheaper seats clap their hands. The rest of you, just rattle your jewellery." The Queen Mother smiled.

The British *Sunday Times* called Lennon and McCartney "the greatest composers since Beethoven". Not to be outdone, the classical music critic of *The Times* raved about their "pandiatonic clusters" and "flat submediant key switches". Lennon recalled: "It was great. We were kings and at our prime. Harrison added: "We were really tight as friends. That was the good thing about being four together – not like Elvis. Nobody else knew what he felt like. For us, we all shared the experience."

But the Fab Four were about to ascend to even greater heights of fame. As McCartney said: "One of the cheekiest things we ever did was to say to Brian Epstein (their manager) we're not going to America till we've got a No. 1." Unlike any previous British stars, their wish was fulfilled. "I want to hold your hand" did it just before they were given a tumultuous welcome at Kennedy International Airport. During their US tour, they appeared on the *Ed Sullivan Show* – it attracted what is still purported to be the record viewing audience ever in America. No crime was reported for the ten minutes that the Beatles were on the show.

When they flew back to Heathrow Airport in England, they were greeted by huge crowds on the roof of every single building and a huge banner saying "Welcome home boys". The scene has never been repeated. When Lennon was asked on television: "Did your wife enjoy it over there?" he replied: "She loved it. Who? Who?" With typical Liverpudlian humour, Starr chimed in: "Don't tell them he's married. It's a secret."

The song towards the end of the first episode of the Beatles Anthology was apt: "Can't buy me love" which hit No. 1 in March 1964. Although The Beatles went to greater riches and fame in the late 60s, the magic surrounding these four mop-haired young men was never quite the same. But then not even Michael Jackson in his heyday came close.

Johnny Young

But Johnny was pretty gifted too.

21.9.1997 "He could play a guitar like a ring in a bell." That snatch of a song on the radio took me back to my days with Johnny Young, my greatest boyhood chum and fellow pop musician. It all began at Winchester College in September 1957. There I met Johnny who had just taken possession of a Spanish guitar as I had. However, he showed considerably more dexterity on the instrument than anybody else around. He could strum it, pick it, play classical music on it, even do flamenco. He was good.

We formed a school group precociously named "The Aristocats" – three guitars, double bass, drums and washboard – and practised diligently in a classroom off the quad every Sunday morning after chapel. Soon our repertoire had expanded to the point when we gave our first concert in the school armoury of all places. We became a regular feature at the end of every term as we rattled through Lonnie Donegan's skiffle songs like "Rock Island Line" and "Cumberland Gap", interspersing them with Ricky Nelson's "Poor Little Fool", Elvis Presley's "I Need Your Love Tonight" and other rock 'n roll classics. I'd do the singing and Johnny was the lead guitar.

Meanwhile, the two of us obtained vacation work at a coffee bar in Soho, London. We played afternoons and evenings. In April 1963, after leaving school, Johnny and I headed for Paris. We busked on the pavement for the cinema queues and café clientele before striking it lucky as the cabaret for the second-poshest restaurant in the city, L'Auberge Notre Dame. As it was frequented by American tourists flush with dollars, we decided to be French. Thus, when they asked us to sing "The Yellow Rose of Texas", they were amazed that we knew the English words and rewarded us with handsome tips.

Back in England in September 1963, we both went up to Oxford together and entrenched ourselves on the Saturday night bill at the Oxford Union Cellars. By this time, we had purchased primitive amplification equipment and turned ourselves into a dance band. It was a magic atmosphere in those cellars as everybody was jammed in tight and the acoustics were good. Our musical horizon developed beyond the simple three-chord stuff. We started playing Lennon and

McCartney's beautifully melodic compositions like "Michelle" and "Yesterday". But we stuck to what people wanted. Stompers like "Twist and Shout" and "Hippy Hippy Shake" were the real favourites with the audience.

Then it happened. We were given a favourable write-up in "Jennifer's Diary", a social column in a glossy magazine. As a direct result, every debutante in England wanted us to play at her coming-out ball. For two years we criss-crossed the country, entertaining the rich and titled. By day we were studying, by night we were playing. They were crazy times. We were wined and dined and paid extremely well for doing what we loved: getting people to jive on the dance floor.

But in the summer of 1966, a few weeks before our final examinations, the fairy tale ended. Johnny became ill through exhaustion. We never played again together. Johnny had to stay on another year at Oxford to take his Finals while I exchanged the guitar for a suit in the City. Johnny died in 1983. A few Novembers ago, I was having dinner at a restaurant in Cape Town. Seeing a guitar in the corner, the couple I was with asked me to play a few of the old songs. I obliged. The owner of the restaurant came up to me after I'd finished and said: "I don't know who you are but my regular guitarist is going off shortly on his Christmas break. Would you like a three-week contract?" I politely declined but reflected: "Hey, Johnny, we're still current."

Beatrice Webb

And it is fitting that I end off this book with the first article I wrote for the Sunday Tribune *in praise of great-great-aunt Beatrice. She was world class for her time.*

30.10.1994 At the recent Labour Party conference in Britain, it seems as if Tony Blair may have succeeded where Hugh Gaitskell failed in 1959: the scrapping of Clause IV of the Labour constitution. This sacred cow commits the party "to secure for the workers by hand or by brain the full fruits of their industry, and the most equitable distribution thereof that may be possible upon the basis of the common ownership of the means of production, distribution and exchange, and the best obtainable system of popular administration and control of each industry or service".

This clause was drafted by my great-great-aunt Beatrice Webb and her husband Sidney in 1918. She was a remarkable woman of her time, a maverick of the Left with spectacular looks which beguiled Joseph Chamberlain amongst others. As Charles Macaulay wrote to a friend of Beatrice: "Tell her I would give a pretty penny to see her in her crimson satin and white lace dress, but tell her not to be proud of the power of her beauty. It is a grand possession but it has its dangers . . ."

Besides "the clause", she was responsible for the founding of the London School of Economics in 1896 and the *New Statesman* journal in 1913. Her research into the conditions of the slums of the East End of London made her perhaps the first sociologist of note, laying the foundations for much of the subsequent health and welfare legislation in Britain. Not bad for a member of the fairer sex in an era some eighty years ahead of feminism and pleas for gender equality.

In a book entitled *My Apprenticeship* which she inscribed for my mother in 1941, she said the following of her father: "When I was myself searching for a social creed I used to ponder over the ethics of capitalist enterprise as represented by my father's acts and axioms. He was an honourable and loyal colleague; he retained throughout his life the close friendship of his partners; his co-operation was always being sought for by the other capitalists; he never left a colleague in a tight place; he was generous in giving credit to subordinates; he was forgiving to an old enemy who had fallen on evil times. But he thought, felt and acted in terms of personal relationship and not in terms of general principles; he had no clear vision of the public good." Yet she adored her father, looking after him when his health deteriorated in old age to the extent that she nearly collapsed herself.

In later life, her intellectual "general principles" of asceticism led her – together with her husband – into uncritical support of the Soviet Union when it was at its repressive worst. It was an inexcusable error of judgement. All one can say is that it will remain one of the great mysteries of this century that so many intellectuals fell under the spell of Stalin.

In the last entry of her diary on 19 April 1943, eleven days before she died, she wrote: "Suddenly I ceased to exist. We shall all disappear . . . The garden will disappear . . . the earth and the sun and the moon.

God wills the destruction of all living things, man, woman and even a child. We shall not be frozen or hurt, but merely not exist."

Nevertheless, as the Labour Party attempts to modernise itself in its bid to be Britain's governing party on the eve of the new century, her name is regularly recalled in the debate on the party's future direction. There is no doubt that Clause IV should be scrapped because of its association with nationalisation. In its place, though, I would put the following: "to secure for all citizens by hand or by brain the full fruits of their industry and the widest possible ownership of the means of production, distribution and exchange and the best obtainable system of popular administration". The words do not have to be changed that much to exclude the idea of Big Government but to retain the idea that everybody should be rewarded fully for their efforts and have a stake in the economy. South Africa's new constitution needs to reflect a similar sentiment.

We are all creatures of the times we live in. Beatrice saw the complete contradiction between Britain's status as the foremost manufacturing nation on earth and the appalling plight of the destitute – the "people of the abyss" as she called them. She believed that public works programmes and other forms of government intervention would correct the situation. But as Reginald McKenna at the Board of Education said in 1903: "The worst of all your proposals, Mrs Webb, is that though each one seems excellent, they are all more expenditure. And where are we to get the money?" I live in an age which has seen the collapse of the Soviet Union, soaring government deficits through overambitious entitlement programmes and the rise of the dynamic economies in the Far East. I therefore think differently to Beatrice. She believed in redistribution of wealth. I believe in redistribution of skills to create wealth. She believed in equality of outcome. I believe in equality of opportunity. In Britain, she nudged the pendulum towards socialism. In South Africa, I have tried through my "High Road" lectures to nudge the pendulum towards free enterprise.

Forever, mankind will be balancing opposite goals. Every goal may have some validity when considered by itself, but the totality of resources is never sufficient to meet all the goals at the same time. Thus, life will continue to be a constant dialectic – affordability versus the scourge of unemployment, individual enterprise versus a sense of public duty and so on. The arguments will shift this way and that as each generation encounters the same conundrums. But, Beatrice, you did your bit – Clause IV or no Clause IV. I am proud of you. I shall not forget you. You exist for me.

Cover design and typography by Jürgen Fomm
Typeset in 10.5 on 13 pt Palatino and
printed and bound by National Book Printers,
Drukkery Street, Goodwood, Western Cape, South Africa